THEN AND NOW IN BATH'S CHELSEA ROAD AREA

A CHANGING SHOPPING, INDUSTRIAL AND RESIDENTIAL DISTRICT
(OF LOCKSBROOK, LOWER WESTON AND NEWBRIDGE)

*An historical survey
and some personal memories from 1950 -1990
including Newbridge Junior School*

by John Daniels

*With additional material on the history of
The New Crown Inn*
by Penny James
And with contributions attributed to a number of others

THEN AND NOW IN BATH'S CHELSEA ROAD AREA

Copyright © John Daniels and Penny James 2018 All Rights Reserved
The rights of John Daniels and Penny James to be identified as the authors of this work have been asserted in accordance with the Copyright, Designs and Patents Act 1988
All rights reserved. No part may be reproduced, adapted, stored in a retrieval system or transmitted by any means, electronic, mechanical, photocopying, or otherwise without the prior written permission of the author or publisher.

Spiderwise
Remus House
Coltsfoot Drive
Woodston
Peterborough
PE2 9BF

www.spiderwize.com
A CIP catalogue record for this book is available from the British Library.

The views expressed in this work are solely those of the author and do not necessarily reflect the views of the publisher, and the publisher hereby disclaims any responsibility for them.

Chelsea Road 1999

John Daniels SM2 6HR
A Firs Book

CONTENTS

PREFACE - Inspiration and Sources	Page 5
A NOTE ON THE MAPS	Page 7
THE MAPS	Page 9
Geographia Plan of Bath 1949	
JH Cotterell Map of 1852,	
Ordnance Survey Maps 1885, 1903, 1932, 1951, 1963 and 2017	
CHELSEA ROAD AREA HISTORY AND MEMORIES	
1951 Arrival in Foxcombe Road - Chelsea Road as a pivot	Page 16
Transport Links	Page 17
Foxcombe Road	Page 20
A history of Chelsea Road and its beginnings	Page 23
The Horstmann Gear Company (invention and entrepreneurship from Westphalia)	Page 26
Looking around the lower Chelsea Road area (the Post Office etc)	Page 30
A trip up the east side of Chelsea Road (numbers 1-8e)	Page 38
Looking around the upper Chelsea Road area (including Locksbrook Cemetery)	Page 45
Cedric Chivers (and perhaps the greatest Bathonian of the 20th Century)	Page 50
A trip down the west side of Chelsea Road (numbers 9-20): including Kennington Road and Park Road	Page 53
School Days (and a bit of industrial archaeology)	Page 63
The Future of Chelsea Road	Page 76
Conclusion on changes since 1950-1974 (some endings and some new beginnings)	Page 83
NEWBRIDGE JUNIOR SCHOOL	
1956 MRS JONES & 1957 MR HANFF'S CLASSES	Page 87
LANDLORDS OF THE NEW CROWN INN	Page 91
THE HORSTMANN FAMILY	Page 92

CREDITS	**Page 94**
Sources & References	
Acknowledgements	
Picture Credits	
PICTURES OF CHELSEA ROAD 2018	**Page 100**
ANNEXES	
A summary of shops in Chelsea Road	**Page 106**
Census data 1891, 1901 and 1911	**Page 107**
Kellys & Post Office Directories	**Page 108**
1895, 1911 & 1914	
1919 & 1922	
1923 & 1927	
1932 & 1937	
The 1939 Register	**Page 112**
Kellys & Post Office Directories	**Page 113**
1950 & 1963	
Intervening Changes 1950-1963 and 1963-1970	
1970 & 1974	
Transition Report 2012	**Page 117**
2017 Google & Internet & 2018	**Page 118**
The challenges of road numbering	**Page 119**

PREFACE

Inspiration and sources

I began to take an active interest in the history of Chelsea Road and the adjoining roads after seeing a posting on a website by a friend from Newbridge Junior School days, Elizabeth Prevett (nee Baxter). She had posted an extract of the 1970/1 Bath Kellys Directory on a Bathonian's Facebook page. This concerned Chelsea Road and she kindly sent me further extracts for adjoining roads.

I already had a copy of the 1932 Post Office Directory of Bath that had belonged to my grandfather Frank Pine (that I had used in my book about him). I then managed for a modest sum, to buy on discs the Post Office Directory for Bath for 1922 and Kellys Directory for 1950. This has also helped with my family research into Combe Down. I also have acquired on disc extracts from directories for Bath for 1830, 1844, 1856, 1889, 1919, 1923, 1927, 1931 and 1939. Even so, I have not found the latter quite as useful since, apart from the ones for 1919, 1923 and 1927, they do not include a street listing. I am indebted to the Bath Record Office for copies of local maps and Post Office and Kelly's Directories extracts for 1937, 1963 and 1974, and the intervening years, and to Jane Brimble (nee Fudge) for Kellys 1971/2. More recently I have discovered Leicester University's on-line Historical Directories for records from 1895, 1911 and 1914.

I have looked also at the censuses for 1891, 1901 and 1911 and the 1939 Register. The censuses provides a useful street listing for residents but not, in the main, for businesses (except for those living over the shop). That is also generally the case for the 1939 Register although, rather better than the censuses, it does accurately record the ages of those recorded. I have also looked at Bath Chronicle newspapers of the era 1890-1950 that are available online.

It's sad to think that the old Kellys/Post Office Directories that are becoming an increasingly accessible resource in this internet age were killed off in the internet age by the availability of much more fragmented paid-for resources. TV programmes like 'Who do you think you are?' and, more recently, David Olusoga's excellent BBC2 series 'A House Through Time' have highlighted the possibilities of research into families and houses in the internet age. Even so these rely on census data that can only be published 100 years in arrears and that will dry up in 2021 until the 1951 census data is available (the 1931 census data was destroyed by a Second World War bomb and the 1941 census never happened). In any case the Chelsea Road area is generally too recent for much published census data.

Although I have related a few personal anecdotes from the third quarter of the 20th century, this little work is not about tracing individual families. However the lack of Kellys/Post Office Directories after 1974 means that between the late 1970s and 2017 one must rely on personal memories – there is no easily accessible and reliable record. In view of the fact that between 1970 and 1974 some 10 (about a third) of the shops in the Chelsea Road area changed there is clearly scope for considerable change in the space of 40 odd years to date.

TV soaps like 'East Enders' and 'Coronation Street' portray fairly cohesive communities in which everyone knows everyone else. They represent their locations as capsules from which people do not easily escape until they suddenly take a taxi ride to a new home and never appear again – shades of the 1960s TV series 'The Prisoner'! I doubt that anywhere was ever like that, although Foxcombe Road and the roads enclosed by Chelsea Road were a distinct area to which I often return in my mind's eye (a perception sharpened by absence - and therefore offering a focus on a frozen time frame that has not been distorted by the fug of daily life in a particular location). Also I have allowed this narrative to get out and about into the surrounding roads!

The surrounding roads have contained a number of employers whose managers and employees are likely to live and shop in the area so I have taken a look at those major employers that might have had an impact on the area. So I have stretched the boundaries of inquiry to Combe Park, the Locksbrook and Brassmill Lane areas and part of the Lower Bristol Road. The schools in the area are also an important aspect of the character of any district.

I am grateful to Penny James and all the other people who have helped me in this project.

JOHN DANIELS

A NOTE ON THE MAPS

The story of the area can be partly told in a series of maps that, even so, beg questions as to when precisely the changes they depict actually occurred.

Chelsea Road in Context 1949: This 1949 Geographia Plan of Bath illustrates the location of Chelsea Road area in the context of the area west of Bath. This includes Weston Village, the hospitals and the rail network then – particularly the Midland (with its station at Weston) and the Somerset and Dorset lines out of Bath Green Park.

The JH Cotterell Map of 1852: There is virtually no development in the area except for a few houses along what became Newbridge Road.

Ordnance Survey Map 1885: This shows the New Crown Inn and some buildings on the east side of what is now Chelsea Road (numbers 3-8). Apart from 40 houses or villas, Newbridge Road and what was to become Newbridge Hill (then Kelston Road) were both relatively undeveloped, although there was quite a bit of development in Station Road and Locksbrook Road.

Ordnance Survey Map 1903: The whole area is now relatively built up. The New Crown Inn has expanded a little and 1 and 2 Chelsea Road are built, but there are gaps to the north-east of Chelsea Road and on the south side of Park Road. The area west of Foxcombe Road between Newbridge Hill and Newbridge Road is still park land.

Ordnance Survey Map 1932: There are new houses in Park Road, and west of Foxcombe Road there are 2 new villas. Also the Newbridge Works of Horstmann's feeding off Newbridge Road have been well established (the factory was to expand into the area marked as tennis courts).

Ordnance Survey Map 1951: In Chelsea Road the Co-op and two adjacent shops are in evidence, but there is still a gap south of them. Park Road has two new semi-detached houses on the south side, although there are still two orchard plots on the south side, and there is access to Newbridge Works from Park Road. The works have doubled in size and there are buildings along the bottom of Foxcombe Road.

Ordnance Survey Map 1965: There are no gaps in the north-east of Chelsea Raod. Park Road has 4 new semi-detached houses where the orchards were. The Newbridge Works now fills virtually all the land south of the two villas behind Foxcombe Road (that may have belonged to members of the Horstmann family).

Ordnance Survey Map of today: With the closure of the Newbridge Works a small housing estate has been built with access to it from Newbridge Road along Horstmann Close. There are also houses backing onto Horstmann Close with frontages on the lower part of Foxcombe Road that are numbered as a continuation of Park Road. The 2 villas behind Foxcombe Road have been replaced by the sheltered flats of Newbridge Court. Newbridge Primary School has expanded considerably.

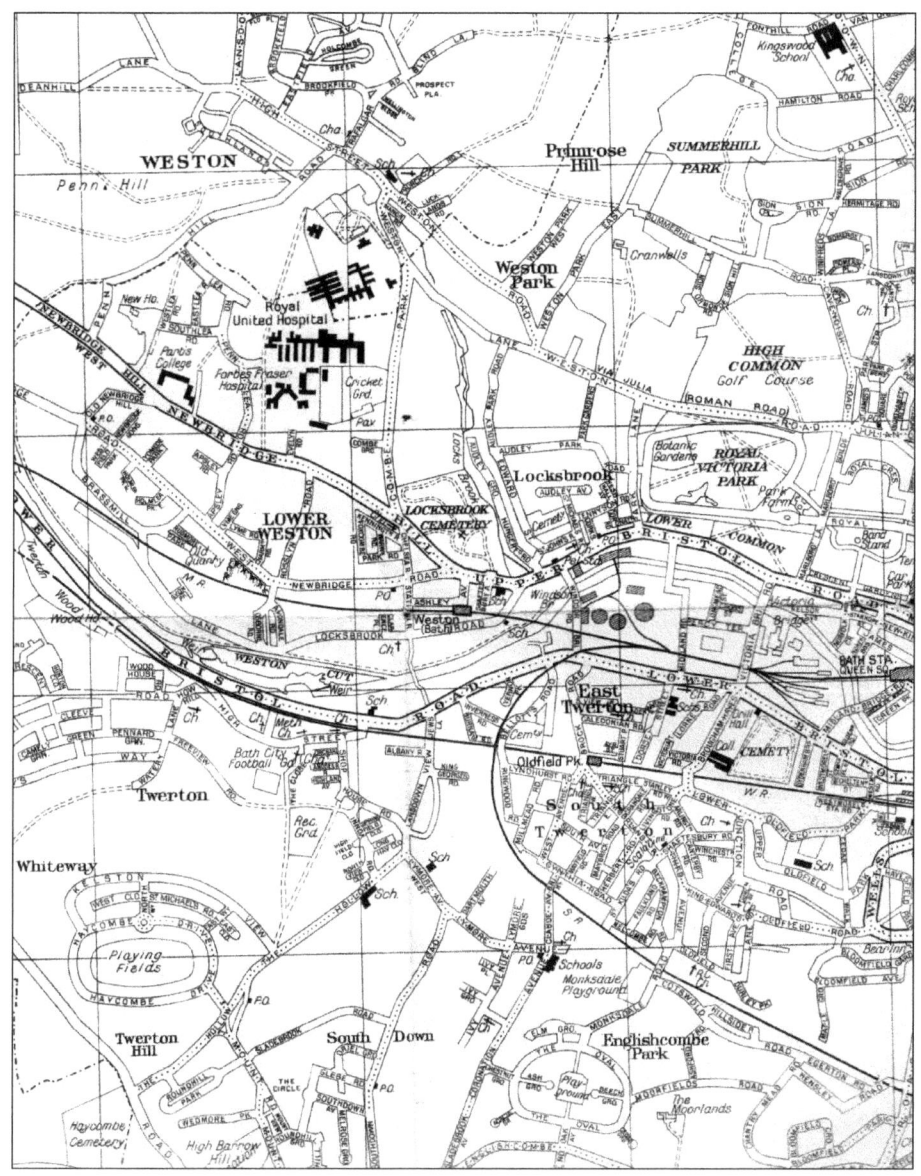

Chelsea Road in context 1949

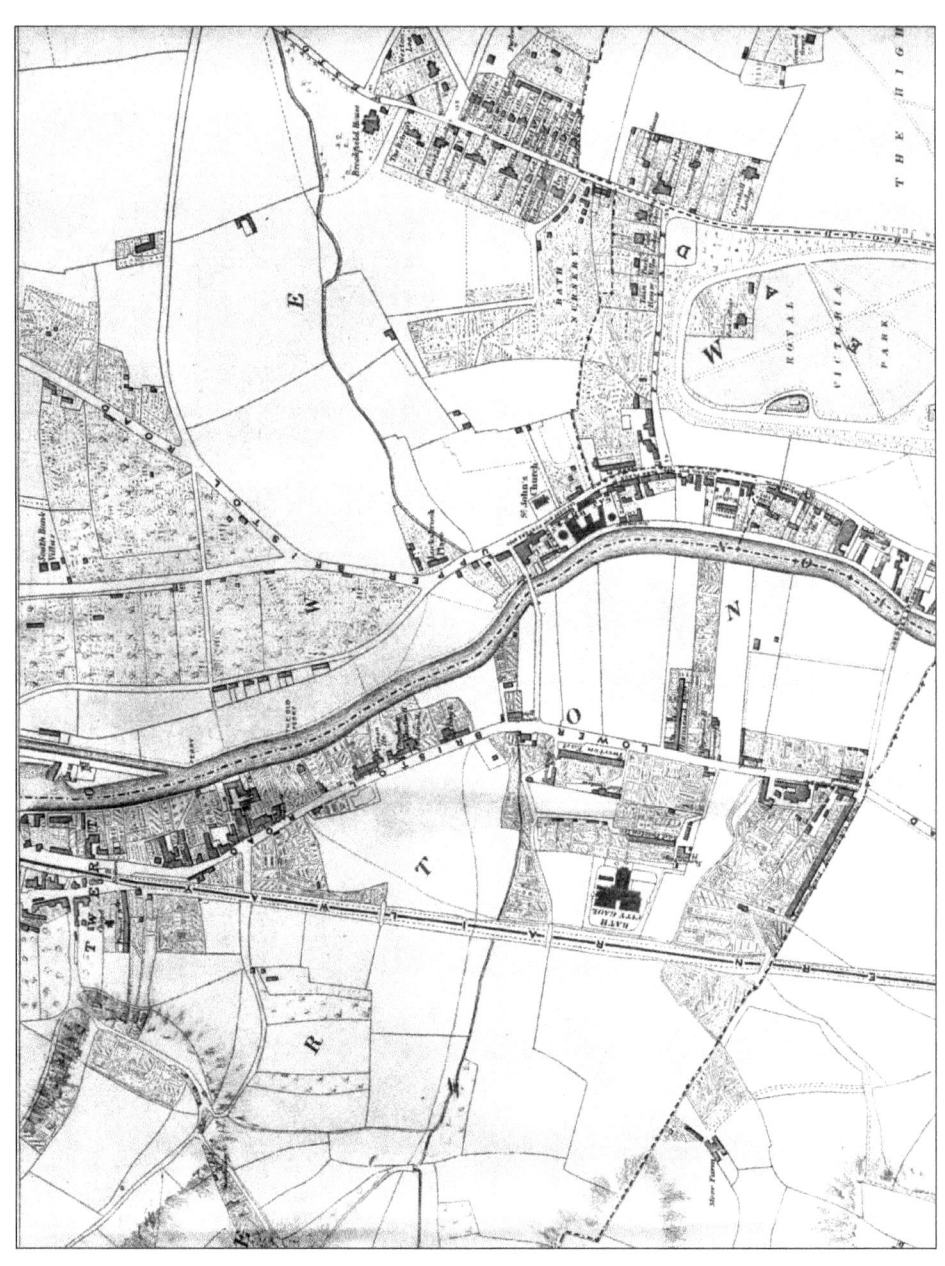

Chelsea Road Area – JH Cotterell Map 1852

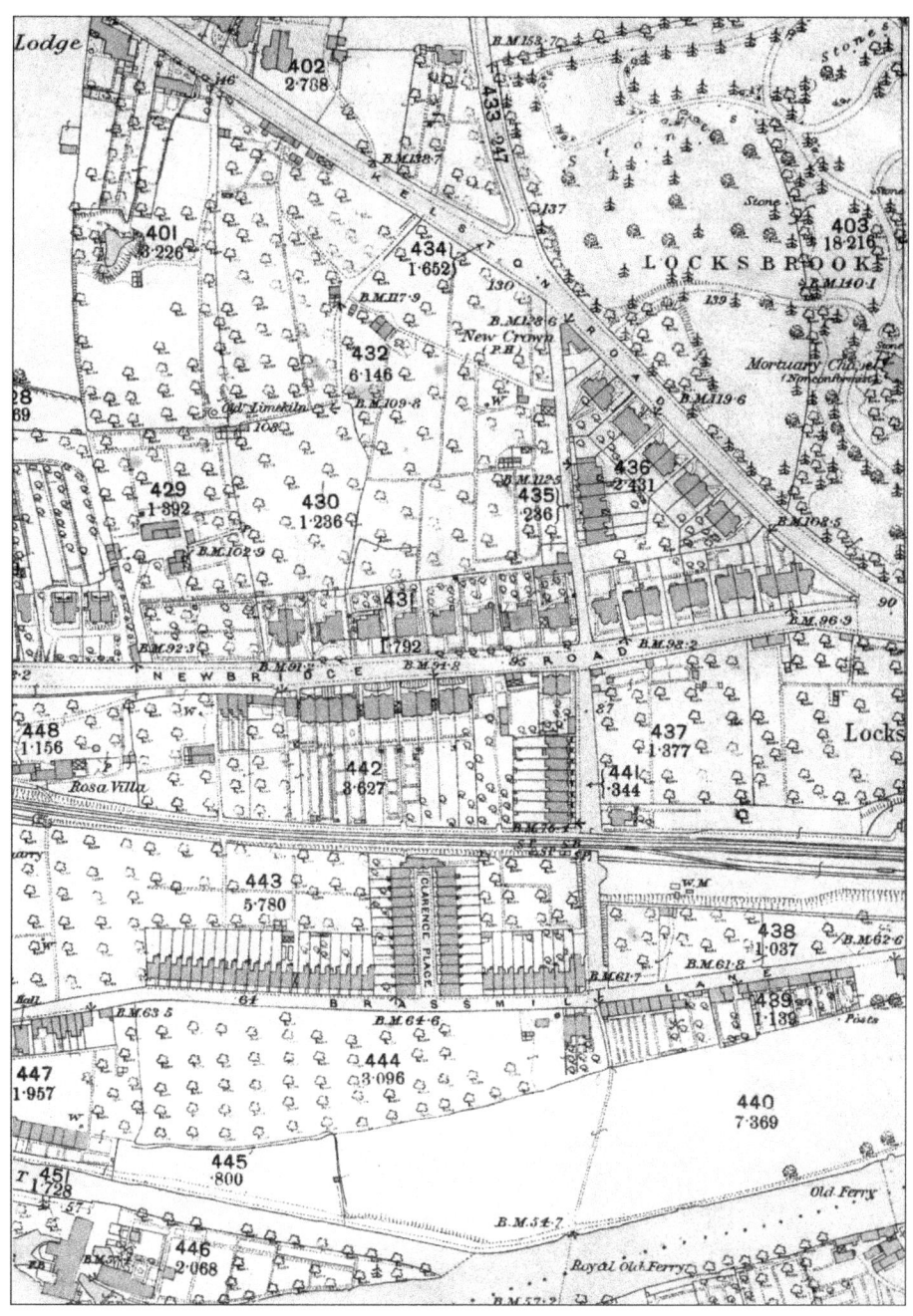

Chelsea Road Area – OS Map 1885

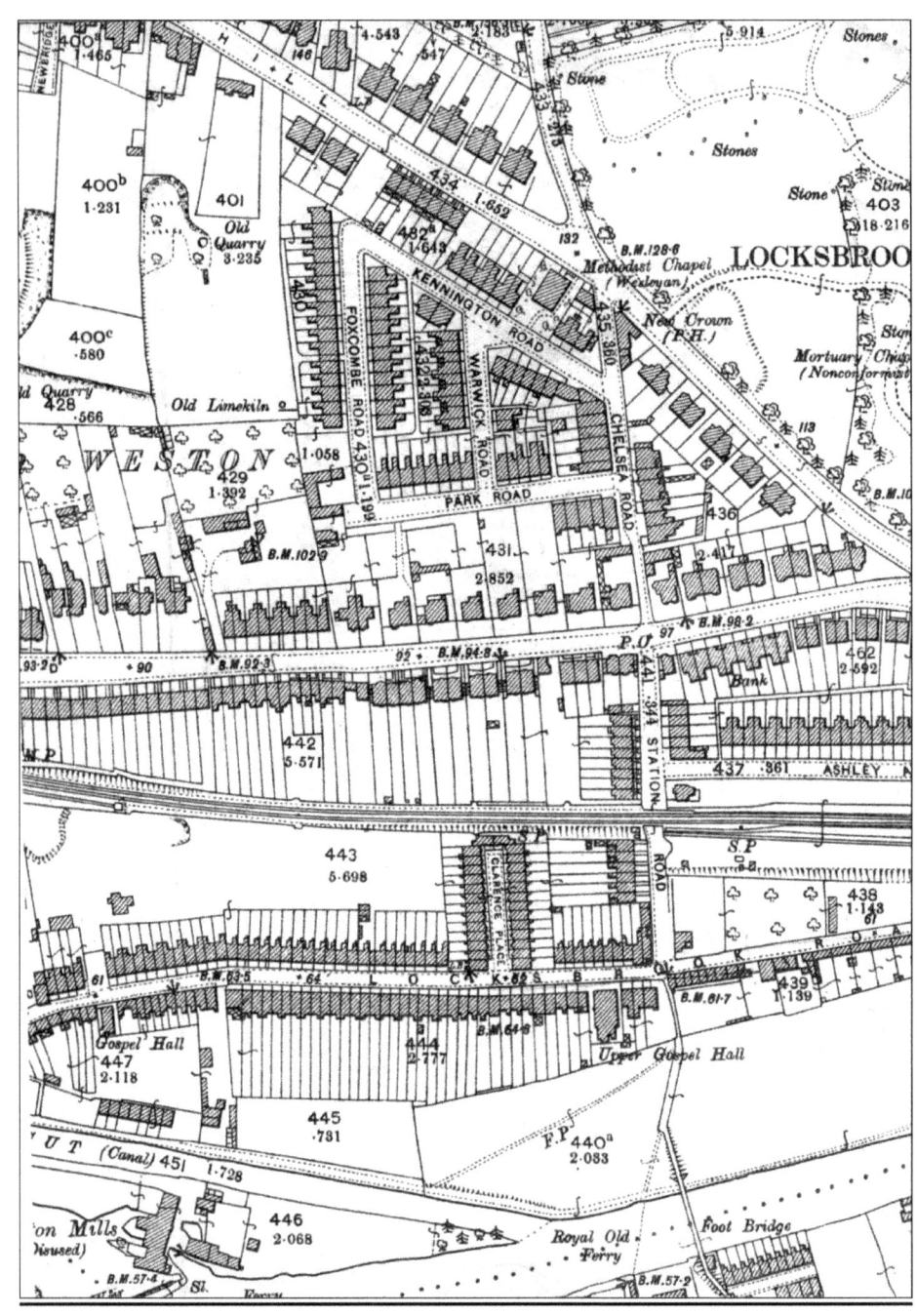

Chelsea Road Area OS Map 1903

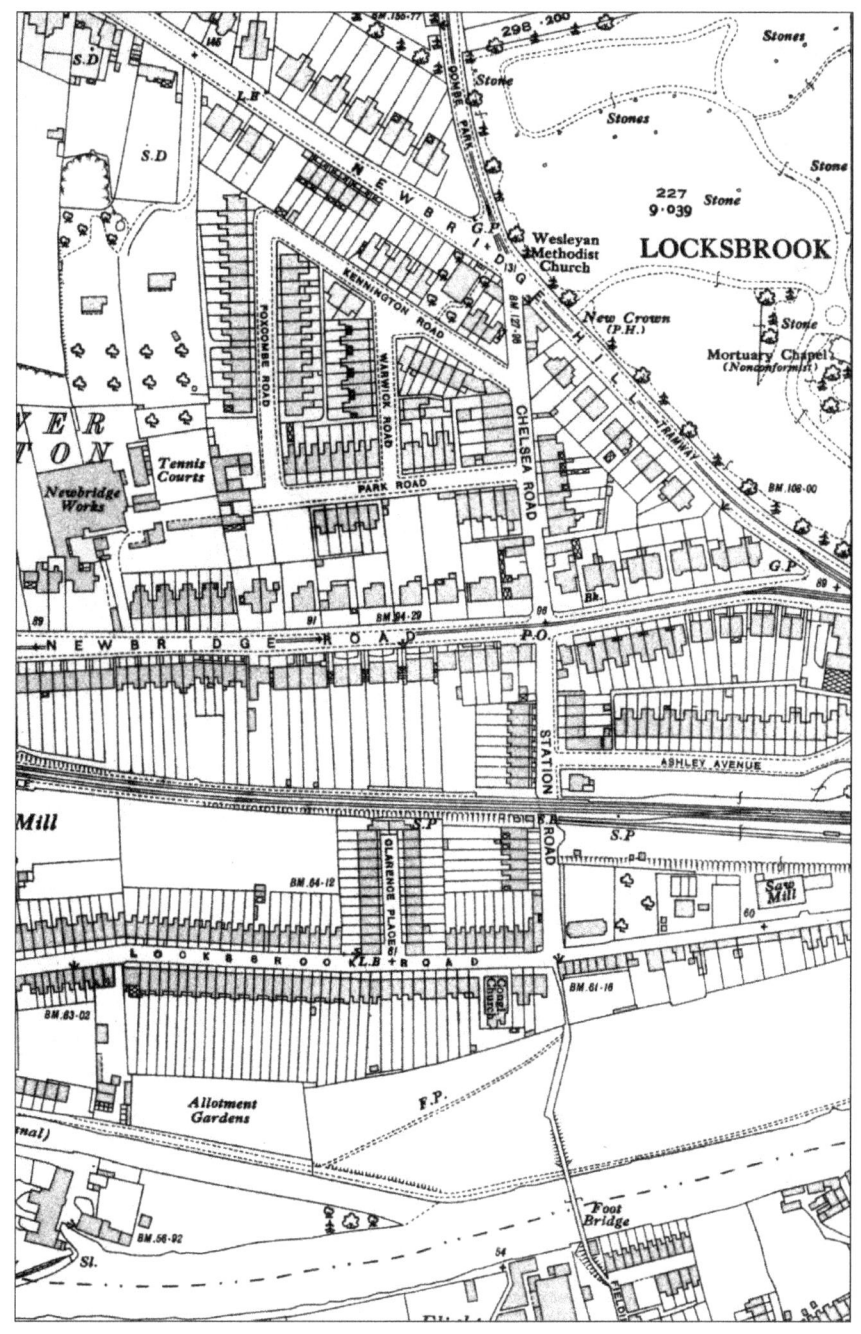

Chelsea Road Area OS Map 1932

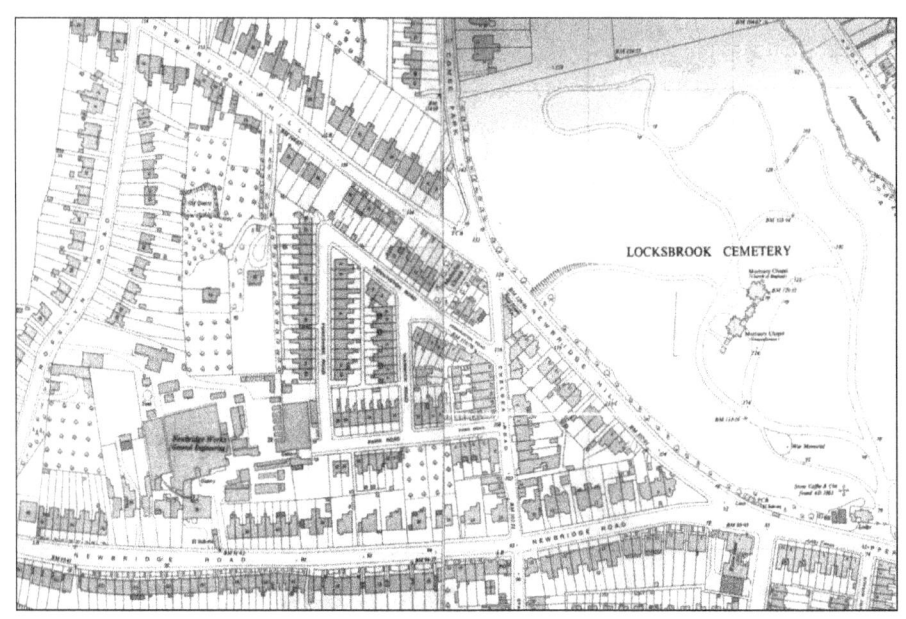

Chelsea Road Area OS Map 1951

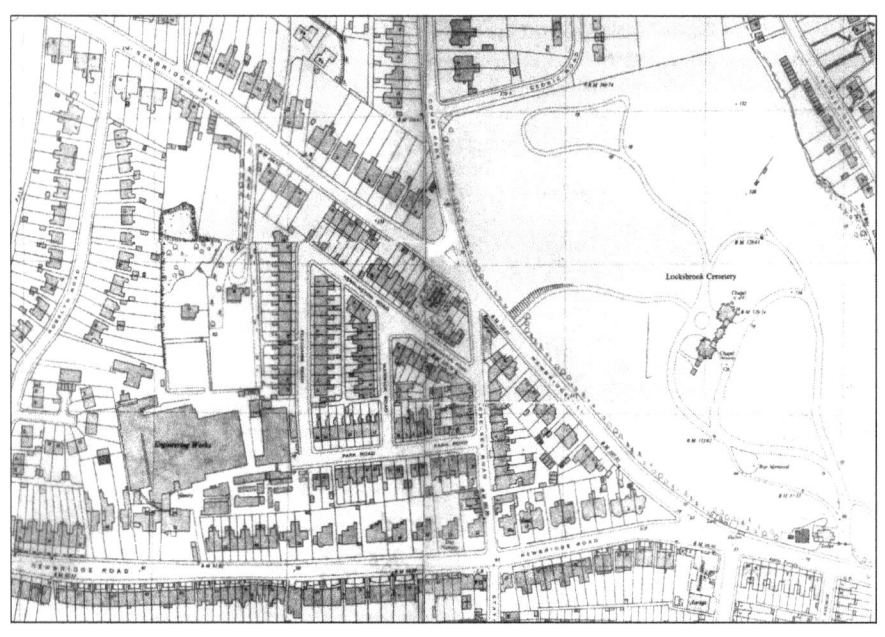

Chelsea Road Area OS Map 1965

Chelsea Road Area today

CHELSEA ROAD, BATH
A CHANGING SHOPPING INDUSTRIAL AND RESIDENTIAL AREA
An historical survey and some personal memories from 1950-1990

1951 ARRIVAL IN FOXCOMBE ROAD – CHELSEA ROAD AS A PIVOT

My story starts with a taxi ride. My father was born in 1913 in Littleton Drew, a village in Wiltshire. His father Worthy was a butcher and his mother Lucy listed her profession as nurse on her wedding certificate at Chippenham Registry Office in 1904. After contracting polio in 1926 my father was nursed back to his feet by his mother who, from 1929, secured him a place to train at the Derwent College for disabled adults in Oswestry founded in 1928 by Dame Agnes Hunt. So my father became a surgical appliance maker. He first worked at Bath Orthopaedic Hospital (with a period at the Cripples Guild in Nottingham in the 1940s). My mother lived most of her early life at 17 The Firs, Combe Down, and they met because my Great Uncle Robert lived at 8 The Firs. My parents married in 1945 - their picture was front page of The Bath and Wilts Chronicle and Herald on VJ day. In 1951 he returned to the orthopaedic workshop now part of the Royal United Hospital at Combe Park, Bath, where in due course he ran the surgical appliance workshop. Returning to Bath with my mother Lena, my brother Roger and me in 1951, we stayed briefly with my mother's sisters (Aunts Phyllis and Edna Pine) at 17 The Firs, Combe Down. Later that year we arrived at 17 Foxcombe Road in a Fale and Ralph taxi from Combe Down.

It is surprising to reflect now on what a pivotal location Chelsea Road was in the 15 years when I was growing up - from 1951 until I went to London University College in 1965 *(my parent's deaths in 1990 and 1991 finally severed my links with the area)*. In those years we shopped there for food, meat, drink, paraffin, medicines etc. In the late 60s, on returning from college or in the 1970s on returning with my wife Carole from Sutton, Surrey, we might go in the evening with my parents for a drink at the New Crown.

I grew up at 17 Foxcombe Road, on the west side of the road, which was located at the end of a pattern of roads that included Kennington, Warwick and Park Roads. This network plugged into Chelsea Road, which was the only way out from these roads - although a few houses in Newbridge Hill backed onto Kennington Road *(one of those houses was that of the Tobin family at 39 Newbridge Road where we went to play with the Tobin twins and a large Trix train set created by John Tobin's uncle who lived with them)*. The houses in this network were built as terraces from about 1895 onwards, with little scope for garages, in the days when motoring was a rich man's luxury. Consequently the roads are now choked with cars - and residents have for many years jostled for on-road parking spaces.

TRANSPORT LINKS

The Chelsea Road area is well-served by public transport. Initially there was the era of horse buses (see picture below of the Newbridge Horse Bus 1890). However, between about 1905 and 1939 (when they were scrapped), there were blue and cream electric trams from the centre of Bath, along the Upper Bristol Road and Newbridge Road to the Globe Inn at Newton St Loe. Another tram route diverted from the Upper Bristol Road at the Weston Hotel (now known as The Weston) and headed up through Combe Park to Weston Village Church. There was a tram shelter, ticket and parcels office at the top of Chelsea Road - across the road from the Crown pub. The Bath in Time website has some Dufaycolor slides of Bath trams in 1937.

The Bath trams changed little in their 34 years of unprofitable operation. With the driver exposed to the elements - and the passengers too on the top of a double deck - the fully enclosed double deck buses that replaced them from 1938 were a step change in comfort. In 1936 the Bristol Omnibus Company took a controlling interest in Bath Electric Tramways Limited and Bath Tramways Motor Company Limited (formed in 1920 as a subsidiary of BET to run the motor bus services). Even after nationalisation of bus services in 1948 Bath bus services were identified (perhaps for legal reasons) as being run by one or other of these companies.

Bath, Newbridge Road.

In the 1960s the 4 and 4a buses were two of a dozen Bath City routes 'operated by' Bath Electric Tramways Limited. They ran from Foxhill Hutments (or, in the case of the 4a, Foxhill Estate), via Midford Road (Cross Keys), the Bear Flat, Kingsmead Square/Westgate Buildings, Combe Park and Weston Village. In the 1950s before the creation of this route there was a number 20 bus that served Weston Village from Bath Spa Station. The number 19 from Bath Spa Station to Kingsmead Square and Newbridge Road was also a BET route. The number 17 bus from Claverton Down to Widcombe Hil, the Parade Gardens, Newbridge Hill and Penn Lea Road was one of a ten Bath City routes 'operated by' Bath Tramways Motor Company Limited. In the 1960s the two country bus routes in the area were the 33 and 33a from Bath via Newbridge Road to Keynsham and Bristol and the 134 from Bath via Newbridge Hill to Bitton and Bristol.

These days First Group Bath buses follow somewhat changed routes. The number 4 goes every 10 or 12 minutes from Upper Weston Eastfield Avenue via Combe Park to the city centre, but after the Bear Flat it terminates on Odd Down. The number 9 travels every hour from the Bus Station to Upper Weston Falconer Road via Penn Lea Road. There are also, travelling along Newbridge Hill, the 19 to Cribbs Causeway via Kelston and the 37 Bath to Bristol via Hanham. Newbridge Road is served by fairly frequent U5 route from the city centre to Bath Spa University and the U6 circular route (Lower Bristol Road, Newbridge Road and the Bath Spa University). There is also the 21 Newbridge Park and Ride and the 19A to Cribbs Causeway via Keynsham plus the 39 and x39 to Bristol via Saltford.

Although I remember using Weston Station, it closed some time before the final closure of the Somerset and Dorset Railway line from Bath Green Park to Bournemouth. Foxcombe Road was much higher up than Newbridge Road so I rarely heard Midland line trains from Bath to Mangotsfield and Bristol that ran behind Newbridge Road. But at night I could often hear steam trains battling their way up the steep climb out of Bath on the S&D that curved around Oldfield Park. The S&D line, now part of the linear park and cycle track, initially headed west then bent south around Bellots Road, as it crossed the GWR line. It then headed south east to the Devonshire Tunnel, Watery Bottom and the Combe Down Tunnel. This second tunnel was a mile long unventilated single track tunnel that often had trains with 3 engines - a double headed train with a banker - passing through it. So smoke often poured out of the entrances at Watery Bottom and Tucking Mill long after a train passed through.

FOXCOMBE ROAD

My parents lived at 17 Foxcombe Road from 1951 until the late 1980s renting from Mr Ken Horstmann. The house was joined by an arch to number 18 (giving an extra upstairs room and a largish L-shaped bedroom). The arch gave access to a fairly wide lane behind the west side of Foxcombe Road that was lined, beyond a fence, by a row of hazelnut trees. In the ground beyond the trees and north of Horstmann's factory was a large house with large grounds. The Ordnance Survey map for 1932 shows two houses at the bottom of a private road, leading off Newbridge Hill, in an area that was previously marked as a quarry. One of those may have been called 'The Shack'. That is where on 26 April 1942, during the Bath Blitz, Mr. Percival F. Horstmann, departmental manager of the Bath engineering firm, his wife, Elsie, and his son and only child Terence (aged 15) were killed in the Sunday night raid. Mr. J. F. Parke, manager of the machine tool section of Messrs. Joseph Pugsley and Sons, of Bristol, and Mrs. Parke, who were with Mr. and Mrs. Horstmann, were also killed.

The Bath Chronicle report noted that Mr. Percival Horstmann was the younger son of Mr. G. O. H. Horstmann, MBE, chairman of the company, and the late Mrs. Eleanor Sarah Horstmann (i.e. the grandson of Gustav Horstmann the founder of the dynasty). A onetime member of the local Round Table, he was also vice-president of Newbridge Male Voice Choir and an enthusiastic member of Bath Beekeepers' Association.

That then is the area where the council and a housing association built Newbridge Court with access from Newbridge Hill (next to our former doctors). This development provided very good sheltered accommodation at affordable rents in individual two bedroom flats. My parents spent the last 2 or 3 years of their lives living comfortably there. My father Herbert died in 1990 and my mother Lena (nee Pine) in 1991. Here they are pictured in 1987 at 17 Foxcombe Road with my wife's parents.

In the 1950s our neighbours at 16 Foxcombe Road were the Pegrums (who moved to Bathampton before returning to Kennington Road some years later). They were followed by the Pullins (with whose children, Carol and John, my brother Roger and I occasionally played). At 18 Foxcombe Road were the Eastaugh family (replaced by the Bairds in the 1960s). Jimmy Eastaugh, the younger son, was a butcher who, I believe, took over one of Mr Jefferis' branches in Oldfield Park. The other son Bobby died aged 74 on 8 January 2018. In the 1950s Mr and Mrs Lewis Reeve lived at 15 Foxcombe Road: he taught at Newbridge Junior School when I was there. In the 1950s, at 20 Foxcombe Road there lived the curate of St John's Church (Revd. Johnson). At the north end of our (west) side of the road the longest residents by the 1950s were the Stevenson family – Sally Stevenson was like a big sister to many of the children in the road: she once blooded her head chopping wood in front of her house. I remember Mrs Hockin at 21 Foxcombe Road and Mrs Hayward at 25 Foxcombe Road - both there in 1950 and 1970.

On the opposite side of Foxcombe Road, at 5 Foxcombe Road, Mr and Mrs Lock lived on the ground floor (he was a porter at the RUH). Mr and Mrs Hucklebridge lived on the upper floor (he was a gardener). She was not very mobile in later years (I used to run errands for her). They were all there in 1950 and were still there in 1970. In 1950 the Perrys (with whom Elizabeth Baxter and her family briefly lived in the early 1950s) were at 7 Foxcombe Road. The Spurrells at 8 Foxcombe Road ran a taxi firm. Also at number 8 were Raymond and Richard Tallon. Other families familiar to me in the 1970 directory are the Tugwells, Bolwells and Vowles at 7, 8 and 9 respectively.

Apart from the Chelsea Road shops there were deliveries of milk by Norton Dairies and, I think, the Co-op. My mother had bread delivered by the Co-op – paid for by bread tokens purchased at the shop. There may have been greengrocery deliveries by Hughes Greengrocers (Patricia Hughes was in my class at Newbridge). The Corona lorry came round selling lemonade, orangeade, apple-ade, dandelion and burdock and other drinks in returnable bottles with china stoppers. Elizabeth Prevett (nee Baxter) remembers a rag and bone man who came round with his daughter and their horse and cart. He used to let Elizabeth have a ride on his horse but Elizabeth's mother felt she had to take her in and bath her afterwards!

Then there was Toni Tiani, with his Ice-cream van and his habit of calling cornets 'doorknobs' or 'dornets'. For many years, from the late 1940s until at least the 1970s, the Tiani family had an ice-cream parlour and cafe at 16 Westgate Street, opposite the Beau Nash Cinema. Pre-war, in 1939, they were fruiterers at this address (as they had been in 1931 at 3 Corn Street, where previously they had been confectioners in 1927). However, in 1939, they also ran a milk bar at 3 Lower Borough Walls.

Lastly, in those days you paid for your insurance needs in cash to an agent who collected your payments. We were called upon by William Henry Jordan Shepherd, a

Labour Councillor for Twerton and (from 1964) an Alderman, who was Mayor of Bath in 1961. He was a jolly red-haired man always ready for a chat.

In 1947-8 Mr Shepherd had been Chairman of the Electric Lighting Committee of Bath Corporation. This was the last year before the electricity generation role of Bath Corporation's Electrical Department (the Bath Electricity Undertaking) was handed over on 1 April 1948 to the new Nationalised industry that became the South Western Electricity Board. The last but one Chief Electrical Engineer of Bath (1925-1945) was a Mr Spark!

A HISTORY OF CHELSEA ROAD AND ITS BEGINNINGS

An interesting question is 'when did it become Chelsea Road and when were the east side and the adjoining roads built?' My guess is from the late 1880s onwards. The J Cotterell map of 1852 shows a road where Chelsea Road is now, but with no buildings at all in the area. The road is essentially a short cut to the river ferry (The Royal Old Ferry) and later a foot bridge to Twerton (pictured here).

The Ordnance Survey map of 1885 shows a handful of buildings on the east side of Chelsea Road (more or less where 3-7 Chelsea Road are now) and to the west in

Newbridge Hill (it was Kelston Road then) and some villas in Newbridge Road to the east and west. However to the west of Chelsea Road there was only un-built land. There were some houses in what is now known as Station Road. However the Ordnance Survey map of 1903 shows the whole complex of roads (Kennington Road, Foxcombe Road, Park Road and Warwick Road) completed except for the north east part of Chelsea Road and the southern side of Park Road (except 1 and 2). This was already reflected in the 1895 Post Office Directory.

I am indebted to Penny James, the current land-lady of the New Crown Inn for the following information:

Many years ago, the triangle of land which is now wedged by Chelsea Road, Newbridge Hill and Newbridge Road was owned by Thomas Leir and his son John, who owned a large amount of land in this area. They were gentlemen farmers.

Between 1845 and 1878, they drew up plans to sell the land, which was a market garden with an inn called the Crown. John Beavis was the inn keeper who lived with his wife Mary Anne and their two sons and daughters.

Some of Penny's sources have been a lot of old documents given to her by Ushers of Trowbridge. Penny hasn't been able to establish when the original Crown Inn was built, although she has tried very hard to discover it. It's on the 1851 tithe map. It seems that John Beavis was a market gardener living in the building which became the Crown Inn. Sometime in the 1850s he started to sell beer and opened his home as a beer house, which was allowed in those days. He must have named it The Crown, not very original! He carried on doing this until the family moved into The New Crown in 1878. Not long after that the property became fully licensed to sell spirits. In 1878, after it and its surrounding land was sold for £1,850, the old inn was demolished and a new Crown Inn was built, along with the ten villas at Newbridge Hill. It was a coaching inn between Bath and Bristol.

The original New Crown was smaller than the present building as the stable block was added in the 1890s when Arthur Beavis was the Landlord. Incidentally, Arthur was married to Elizabeth Bright King who was the daughter of Thomas Bright King, the landlord of The Full Moon at Twerton. She has provided a list of publicans at The New Crown, which is annexed.

On May 30th 1897, John Beavis bought the brand new Crown Inn for £649. He borrowed £504 with a mortgage to be repaid over 688 weeks (roughly 13 years) at a rate of £1 and 2 shillings per week. Unfortunately, John died on 7th November 1897 and Mary Anne took over the running of the inn and stables. John is buried in Locksbrook Cemetery but is he the ghost that has been sighted several times at the inn? There is also a child ghost with blonde curls that has been spotted several times but we have no idea who he could be.

In October 1880, Mary Anne sold the New Crown Inn to Thomas Bright King but it seems the inn was still run by the Beavis family. Arthur, John and Mary Anne's son, was landlord until 1886, when it was taken over by his son Arthur W Beavis. In 1891, Arthur W. Beavis bought the inn back and continued as landlord until 1903 when he sold it to William Withers and retired to 121 Newbridge Road where he lived until 1925. William Withers owned the Larkhall Inn and, in 1925, went into partnership as Pearce, Reynolds and Withers and, trading as The County Brewery, changed the name of The New Crown Inn to The Crown Brewery but it is not clear if brewing was actually done on the premises. In 1911, The Crown Brewery was sold to Georges of Bristol and, in 1931, the name reverted to The New Crown Inn.

Courage's brewery took over Georges in 1961 and the inn stayed as a Courage house until the late 1980s when it was transferred to Ushers of Trowbridge (newly independent of Watney's) in an anti-monopoly pub swap. When Ushers ceased trading in the mid 1990s The New Crown Inn was managed by the pub company Innspired Inns until 2005 when it was taken over by Punch Taverns, the largest pub company in the UK.

The evidence of the Kellys/Post Office Directories is that Chelsea Road was still incomplete in 1919: the north end of the east side of the road had still to be built (south of the New Crown - what is now 8-8e including the old Co-op site). Although these directories do not all give a full residential listing, the 1922 Post Office Directory does, and it shows Kennington Road, Foxcombe Road, Park Road and Warwick Road as completed. The exception was that that the odd numbers from 9-21 Park Road remained to be built. This was still the case in 1932 and 1950, although by the 1970 Kellys, 9-15 Park Road had been built (as modern semis rather than terrace houses – so eliminating the prospect of 17-21 being built). By 1950 numbers 35 and 37 had been built close to the junction with Foxcombe Road (which was the main works entrance of the Horstmann Gear Company). I remember these houses going up and also the workers spilling out into Park Road when the works siren went off at the end of the working day. Park Road was completed more recently with houses 39-43, where the entrance to Newbridge Works had been, and 45-55 going up Foxcombe Road!

It is possible that the Horstmann family owned properties in the area with a view to the expansion of their Newbridge Works: my parents at 17 Foxcombe Road were tenants of Ken Horstmann (1903-1973 - he was the grandson of Gustav Horstmann and the son of Albert Horstmann and latterly lived at 14 Park Lane). In the early 1960s at a works open day I cut my thumb on a ride-on model railway - I still bear a sensitive scar! In the late 1960s I did a holiday job at the factory making trip levers for street lamp clocks. They also had premises opposite the allotments by the Victoria Park called the "Albion Works". The Horstmann Gear Company was a major manufacturer in Bath, but in 1994 the Horstmann family sold out after 140 years, and in the year 2000 manufacturing moved to Bristol. With the closure of the Newbridge Works a whole new housing estate was created in Horstmann Close that decants into Newbridge Road.

THE HORSTMANN GEAR COMPANY (INVENTION AND ENTREPRENEURSHIP FROM WESTPHALIA)

In a history of the Chelsea Road area one needs to say something about the Horstmann Gear Company and the Horstmann family. Apart from their Newbridge Works many of the family lived in the area. Six are listed at various addresses in the Newbridge Hill and Newbridge Road area in the 1932 Post Office Directory. The founder of the dynasty was Frederick Gustav Adolph Horstmannn, who was born in 1828 in Westphalia, Germany. He came to England about 1850 eventually moving to Bath about 1855 and setting himself up as 'Gustav Horstmann, Watch and Clock Maker, and Jeweller'. He married Louisa Knott in 1853 and they had five sons (Gustav Otto, Frederick, Ernest Hermann, Albert and Sydney - see the picture below of them in 1910) - and three daughters (Ida, Augusta and Pauline).

In 1856 Gustav won a prize 'to devise the most accurate and foolproof device to measure the smallest item'. This was a micrometer able to measure items as small as 1/10,000 of an inch and the original is at the Science Museum. He made several self-winding regulator clocks and one is on display at the Museum of Bath at Work. Later the company became 'G. Horstmann & Sons'. Gustav Horstmann died in April 1893 aged 64 with around one hundred patents to his name.

After 1900 Horstmann's Control Business developed into a thriving retail and clock making business. A clockwork gas controller was introduced for the automatic control of street lighting for the Bath Gas and Coke Company. In 1904 Gustav's sons founded the Horstmann Gear Co Ltd. to develop a variable speed gear-box that

Sidney Horstmann (the younger of Gustav's sons) had invented for cars and motorcycles. That year the production of the gas controllers was transferred from G Horstmann and Sons to the Horstmann Gear Co Ltd. The brothers patented the Solar Dial in 1904 which automatically adjusted lighting times at dusk and dawn throughout the year. It was in 1914 that Horstmann started making screw and limit gauges for military production, becoming a leading UK Gauge manufacturer until the business was sold in 1990.

Sidney Horstmann's innovative variable gearbox was not very successful, but he went on to make cars in Bath - producing Horstmann Cars between 1913 and 1929 (the number produced varies from 1500 to over 2000 according to different accounts). Around ten of the cars still exist (including, in this photograph, the 1914 model in The Museum of Bath at Work). The Post office Directory for 1932 still listed Horstmann Ltd, Motor Manufacturers, at James Street West in 1932.

The business eventually became Horstman Defence Systems Ltd (part of the Harris Watkins Group since 2001) and it still exists with offices at 45 Locksbrook Road Bath BA1 3A - designing and manufacturing suspension systems, gearboxes, auxiliary power units, high precision torpedo parts and naval instrumentation. The current Horstman site in Bath occupies over 4,000 square meters and employs over 100 personnel. It is located next to the former Herman Miller factory.

The Newbridge Works was opened in 1915 behind two houses occupied by members of the family in 92/93 Newbridge Road. The property was owned by various members of the family, indeed 2 unmarried female members of the Horstmann family were listed at 92 Newbridge Road in 1932. The block containing the Conference Room and Board Room consisted of the 2 houses once occupied by members of the Horstmann family. The site covered about 4½ acres. The trade name "Newbridge" was then used on most of Horstmann's products. The company occupied the site for more than 85 years until in 2000/2001 the site was sold for housing.

The post Great War slump caused diversification into new products such as gardening tools (the Dandy Dibber), domestic clocks and mousetraps (for Woolworths). The main markets continued in street lighting controls, gas ignition, time switches and gauges. G Horstmann & Son's retail business in Union Street closed in 1925 ending 41 years on the premises and 73 years as watchmakers, jewellers and retailers. It was probably a good company to work for, given the number of pictures of their Works Socials in the Chronicle and Herald Weekly in the 1920s.

The company continued to innovate with products such as the Gas Pistol attached to gas cookers for lighting the oven or cooking rings, which used a battery and glow coil igniter to light the gas. In 1939 they introduced the first system for timing central heating. Horstmann were leading players in the gauge market, street lighting market, and the domestic gas controls market and exported throughout the world.

After 1939 the company was put on a war footing with many products being restricted and gauges prioritised. New war production included the Astro compass, mine switch clock, and radio transmitter for aircraft direction finding. During the war women like Elizabeth Prevett's mother were conscripted from far and wide to work there.

Horstmann first became involved in energy control products in the 1950s and during the next two decades developed an extensive range of central heating programmers and time switches. For a time they had subsidiary companies in India and Australia. The 1960s marked the peak of the Horstmann family's role in managing the business. Although some non-family directors were appointed, the family always dominated and during this period there were ten family members involved: six of the third generation and four of the next generation. In the 1970s Aish and Company Ltd. of Poole was acquired, who specialised in marine equipment. In the late 1980s Horstmann acquired a controlling interest in Serck Controls Ltd.

In 1994 after 140 years of close family involvement, the Horstmann family sold their remaining interest in the business in 1994, and Horstmann Group became part of Clayhithe plc. Clayhithe plc including the Horstmann Group was acquired in 1998 by the measurement and controls group Roxspur plc. In 2000 the business relocated from Bath to new purpose built premises in Bristol with lean manufacturing techniques and some manufacturing functions outsourced. A Management Buy Out was completed in July 2001 and Horstmann Controls became an independent private company. Production of Horstmann Heating and Hot Water Controls continues and are sold at Screwfix and others.

LOOKING AROUND THE LOWER CHELSEA ROAD AREA

There are many interesting things to note and stories to be told about the district. The shopping area of Chelsea Road has one shop that has remained unchanged in the last 100 years – the Post Office and stationers at 41 Newbridge Road (before the late 1930s it was numbered 19). It is on the 1903 map but I can find no record of the Post Office and the adjoining premises in Newbridge Road in the 1901 census. In the 1891 census Richard Canterbury (Baker) and his family were at the Post Office at 6 Augusta Place, Upper Bristol Road. In 1901 they were at their bakers shop at 3 Chelsea Road. Here is a picture from the 1960s when K & PD Beaumont were the proprietors. In 2016 the Post Office was under threat of closure. Currently it offers stationery, party supplies, dry cleaning and shoe repairing. The previous proprietors of the Post Office included in 1895 W Curtiss, and from 1911 until after 1922, Richard Bennett; in 1932, WT Furness; in 1937, Arthur Price; in 1950 George Leslie Mayne; and by 1963 until 1974 and later, K & PD Beaumont. In 1985 they were C & AW Green.

The place next door to the Post Office at 43 (formerly 20) Newbridge Road was Wards the grocers until about 1910 but it was Webbs the grocers for over 40 years from at least 1911 into the 1950s, before becoming Child's grocers. Jim Ironside remembers that, In the mid 1970s, it became Avondale Carpets, until in 1984 Avondale moved to their present site just off Kingsmead Square when the premises became, as it is now, Andrews Estate Agents. The picture below on the left is from

1909 when Richard Bennett had the Post Office and the grocers shop was Wards. The picture on the right is from August 2018.

On the other side of the Post Office, on the corner of Station Road at 39 (formerly 18) Newbridge Road was a small shop that in 1911 and 1922 was Shorney's greengrocers but by 1932 it was Pontings the Chemists – and so it remained into the 1950s. In 1970 and 1974 number 39 was Organ, Kelly & Ewance, chemists. In 1985 it was the Weston Pharmacy. For a while it was the premises of the dog groomers who later relocated to their present shop in Station Road as 'Millionhairs'. More recently number 39 became the Bath Clockworks but in February 2018 it was up for sale.

To the east of Station Road, also on the south side, at 37 Newbridge Road (originally 17) is the Old Red House which (having been an antiques shop) is now a B&B. Iconic but not old (it must have been built in the mid 1930s) it reflected the growing fortunes of Bath baker and confectioner Albert Taylor in the 1920s and 1930s (they catered for my Aunt Connie Pine's wedding on Combe Down in 1938). Still trading in 1974 at 37 Newbridge Road, the company rapidly waned thereafter. In 1939 their main base was 6, 8 and 9 New Bond Street, Bath, with other branches in 31 Rivers Street, 37 Newbridge Road, a factory at 90 and 92 Walcot Street and the Glass House Café, Combe Down. Kellys Directory of Bath for 1971/2 has the following entry: 'Taylor Alfred (Bath) Ltd, 8 & 9 New Bond Street, 37 Newbridge Road & (factory) 90 & 92 Walcot Street'.

Apart from 3 Chelsea Road (where there has always been a bakers) there was another bakers, Hiskins, at 73 (originally 35) Newbridge Road from the First World War until the late 1960s. They were not there in 1970, and their interesting shop front has long gone too - replaced by an ordinary house. Below is a picture of the shop in 1963 and one of Mr and Mrs Hiskins - and the building that has replaced their shop.

I am indebted to Peter De'Ath for the following pictures from the bottom of Chelsea Road in 1905 (and below from about 1915/16). In the first picture from 1905, the various premises are not easy to determine. Both 2 and 3 Chelsea Road appear to be advertising Cadbury's chocolate and cocoa. No 2 appears to be the premises of E Weare, no 3 would be Canterbury's bakers. In the centre is what looks like a post or telegram boy. A boy on the left has a cart from Ward's Stores, which was next to the Post Office in Newbridge Road. Behind him the corner shop is clearly George Read's draper's shop (as it was from before 1901 until after 1911).

In the picture below (from 1915/16) the doctor's premises at 113 Newbridge Road can be clearly seen on the right, and Loveless' Chemists at 112 Newbridge Road on the left. As the latter is now 20 Chelsea Road I will deal with that at the end of my tour up and down Chelsea Road.

The picture below is also supplied by Peter De'Ath. It shows the road in 1908 with G Harrisson's tabacconist at 1 Chelsea Road and K Lucas (probably a greengrocer) at number 2.

By comparison the picture below is from 2012 with Bath Embroidery Services at number 1 and the parent business Regency Cleaners at number 2. I am indebted to Bath Transitions for this picture.

Lloyds Bank (where I first banked on going to university in 1965) was established by the 1920s at **18 (pre-war 114) Newbridge Road**: it was a considerable benefit to local shoppers and traders - but it had gone by 2017 and it is now an office! Next door at no **20 (formerly 113)** was a doctor's surgery from before 1895 until the 1950s). In 1963 its character had changed and it was the premises of car dealers: Specimen Autos, and then in 1970 Newbridge Motors. It then became Roberts News, newsagents. By 1993 it was called The Kiosk. More recently it was been occupied by the charity shop of Dorothy House but in February 2018 it was vacant. It is now the 'Rooted Café'. At **20b Newbridge Road** with premises facing onto Chelsea Road is 'Naughty but Nice' hair salon. From about 1961 this was the original premises of the Regency Dry Cleaners.

Further down at **10 Newbridge Road** was our dentist Fritz Salomon, a Jewish émigré from Nazi Austria who was, at the age of 40, established there by 1939, according to the 1939 register. He was still there in 1974. I recollect that his shaking hands holding a drill were not conducive to a response to his 'open a leettle vider please'.

There have been several hairdressers in the Chelsea Road area over the years. I used to go to the cheaper Mr Woodham's in Station Road to have my hair cut. That is where I first encountered the older clientele being asked 'anything for the weekend sir?' before he reached for a packet of Durex from a display framing the mirrors. The shop is now part of a veterinary surgery - next door is the Genesis gym. Until the closure of the former Mildland Railway line (Bath Green Park to Bristol and Mangotsfield) in the mid 1960s, Station Road was bisected by a level crossing.

Also on the east side of Station Road, north of Woodhams, but south of the level crossing, was Jobbins the Coal Merchant until after sometime after 1974. The 1911 Census lists Charles Jobbins (aged 64), living with his wife and 4 daughters at 8 Station Road, as a Retired Station Master and Coal Merchant (he was a Coal Merchant in the 1911 and 1914 directories). He was the Station Master in 1895 but in 1911 Edmund Redman was Station Master. In later years one of his daughters may have run the coal business. The coal yard was to the west of Weston Station (on the midland line from Bath Green Park to Mangotsfield and the north, and to Bristol). I am indebted to John Alsop for the pictures on the following page - the first from some time before 1910, the second from about 1932.

On the south west side of the line there was a signal box to control the level crossing gates, which is probably the vantage point for the first picture (looking eastward). This shows the relatively short up platform, accessed from the level crossing – half the length of the down platform on which the stone built station building was built. The siding on the right served Jobbin's Coal Yard. The second picture (looking westward) is from the other end of the station and the signal box can be seen in the distance. The station opened in 1869 but closed to passenger traffic in September 1953.

I do remember a trip to Weston-Super-Mare from this station, changing at Bristol Temple Meads. The route to Bristol from Bath Green Park (less than a mile away) went via Bitton, Oldland Common, Warmley and Mangotsfield to Staple Hill and Fishponds and could take 38 minutes or longer. In 1890 there were 12 up and 12 down trains a day calling at Weston (with 2 each way on Sundays). The Sunday service was withdrawn in 1930 and in 1948 there were 11 up and 10 down trains a day. After the closure of the Somerset and Dorset line in 1966, all regular traffic ceased on the line through Weston and the signal box closed in 1968. Some coal traffic continued to Bath Gas Works until 1971 when the gas works closed, and the track was lifted in 1972. The old station is now offices having briefly hosted Bath FM radio station.

North of the level crossing, and leading to the station booking office, is Ashley Avenue. On the north corner of Ashley Avenue, at **18 Station Road**, there was - for many post-war years - an off licence. In 1914 it was the premises of Cecil Burston , beer bottler. It is now 'Millionhairs' devoted to dog grooming (who were previously at 39 Newbridge Road). From the 1950s until after the 1970s one of the teachers at Newbridge Junior School, a Mrs Sybil Jones, lived at **29 Ashley Avenue** (she later moved to Rosslyn Road). After the station, and a lane that led to the back of the old Weston St John's Infant's school, Ashley Avenue loops round to the Weston Hotel.

The Weston Hotel has been known in recent years as 'The Weston'. It re-opened in May 2018 after refurbishment (and with a new manager). I understand it was originally built in the 1880s as a temperance hotel. In the 1920s and well into the 1970s it hosted a number of social gatherings, including weddings and dances and political and other meetings.

In 1922 at **4 Station Road** lived a Mr HF Fiddes a Gas Company collector (presumably with his wife and family). I am sure he was a representative of the Hearts of Oak who sat on the Committee of the Bath Council of Friendly Societies. This committee was chaired by my grandfather Frank Pine from 1922 onwards and was instrumental in saving the Royal United Hospital from debt (see my book 'The Search for Frank Pine'). In 1939 (aged 68) Henry Fiddes was living at **17 Newbridge Road** with his wife Louisa (68) and daughter (39) and son (36), also named Louisa and Henry. He recorded himself as a '(Retired) Friendly Society Counsellor'. In 1950 a Mrs Louisa Fiddes was living at 32 Newbridge Road.

A TRIP UP THE EAST SIDE OF CHELSEA ROAD

In 1908 a photograph shows this was a tobacconist run by G Harrisson. He was listed in the directories as follows: in 1895 as a watchmaker, in 1911 as a jeweller, tobacconist and motor agent. In 1914 it was the premises of Reginald Bainton, Hairdresser. For the years from 1919, if not before, until 1950 and later, 1 Chelsea Road was managed by a Mr Collins, listed either as a hairdresser (in 1922, 1932 and 1937) or a tobacconist (in 1919, 1923, 1927 and 1950) - he was probably both. In 1952 Edward Greenland was the hairdresser here to be succeeded by Ernest L Morris by 1957. By 1961 it was a confectioner and newsagent called 'The Chocolate Box' run by a Major Skuse (where Elizabeth Previtt bought the Chronicle and Herald 'Pink Un' Saturday sports results paper for her father). By 1965 it was Johnson's newsagents before becoming, in 1974, A Philip menswear. More recently it hosted an embroidery business linked to the Regency Cleaners - but along with 2 Chelsea Road it has, since 23 December 2016, been up for sale. It was one of 6 properties for sale in the area in February 2018.

For many years **2 Chelsea Road** was a greengrocer. This address is listed in the 1901 census but, not surprisingly, no residents are recorded. In 1895 it was the shop of William Brice, boot maker. Photographs indicate that in 1905 E Weare was the proprietor and in 1908 it was K Lucas. In 1911 it was occupied by Ward & Co, who also had the shop next to the Post Office at 20 Newbridge Road. It was a greengrocer in 1919 and 1922 run by Edward Banks. Still a greengrocer it was run by EN Rule & Sons in 1932 and Dolman Bros in 1950. I knew the shop as Ganes. They were there from about 1952 until 1996. Here is a picture of Mike Gane and his wife Ann on their last day of trading in 1996.

More recently it became the Regency Cleaners, a branch of the Bath Steam Laundries established in 1897, based in the Lower Bristol Road. After 23 December 2016 it went up for sale (and was still for sale in February 2018).

There has always been a baker's shop at **3 Chelsea Road**: for many years, from before 1895 and well into the 1960s, it was Canterbury's (who had started off at the Post Office, then at 6 Augusta Place). It had a bakehouse at the back (Bridget Johnson - nee Mathews – remembers the smell of fresh bread and the queues to buy it). Then by 1963 it was Burris, bakers – Jane Marshall remembers them selling Neilson's Canadian Ice Cream. From about 1968 it was Homebake (Bath). Here is a picture of the shop in about 1970 and Mr Burris outside his shop in 1985.

Joyce Jones, who has lived behind the bakery shop since 1985, currently owns 3 and 4 Chelsea Road. These properties were purchased by her father David Herbert in 1985 from Mr. Burris, who traded as 'Homebake' until 1985. He bought the business and traded as 'David Herbert, Bread Baker'. Joyce and her late husband (David Jones) took it over in 1990, at which time they changed the name to 'Bath Bakery'. Joyce's husband died in 2001 and she continued to run the business until 2011 when she sold it. It continued to trade as Bath Bakery until it went into administration at the beginning of January 2017. Parsons acquired no 3 straight away and has been trading successfully since. Joyce moved the bakery off-site in 2007, and from this time no 3 remained the bakery shop and no 4 became a separate unit that has been occupied by 'Mercy in Action' charity shop since that date.

Above are pictures from 1985 of the Herberts moving in and David Jones fixing the awning (the Bath Cabinet makers can be clearly seen in the background). On the next page are pictures from 1987 and 2009 of the premises.

For many years **4 Chelsea Road** was a butcher's shop. In 1891 until 1922 and later it was John Henry Butler who ran it until by 1927 a Walter Edward Davey took over. From at least 1932 until well into recent times (after 1974) it was Jefferis before being taken over by Mr Burris. Now (as noted above) it is a charity shop. In 1939 and in 1950 Jefferis had other shops at 18 St Peter's Terrace, Lower Bristol Road and 27 Moorland Road, Oldfield Park. The Jefferis family lived at 38 Newbridge Road, Harold (who I remember as quite breezy) was born in 1906 – he had a cashier called Jerry and there was sawdust on his shop floor. There were 3 butchers in 1950: the others were the Co-op at no 12 (the manager lived over the shop) and Eastmans at no 17 (they were part of a large chain that became part of the Vestey Group in 1922).

From about 1895 until after 1911, **5 Chelsea Road** was the premises of William Rodd, a builder, who in 1911 described himself as a 'speculative builder'. From newspaper advertisements of the time he was something of an estate agent and letting agent. He may well have played a part in the development of the area. The family were still there in 1922. But by 1932 Mr William Byrt had a drapers shop there. I remember in the 1960s Mrs Byrt's old fashioned little haberdashery shop at 5 Chelsea Road, next door to Jefferis, which survived for many years – in 1974 it was Small World, fancy drapers, until after 1985. Martin Pratt has told me that it was subsequently Jack in the Box haberdashers run by Vera Podger who also owned dry cleaners in the road. It is now Interior Harmony Flooring. According to Elizabeth Previtt, Mr Byrt moved to Park Road to live in one of the new semi-detached houses that were built about 1959. They were built on an orchard and garden where Elizabeth and her friends would put bikes against the wall and climb into it to scrump the apples. Once they got caught by Mr Robins the policeman.

The lady who worked behind the counter of Byrt's haberdashers in the 1970s (and possibly before and after that for all I know) was the mother of the actress Patricia Brake. This piece of information came from my friend Philip Russell, whose mother regularly bought knitting wool there. Patricia Brake was born in Bath and after leaving the Bristol Old Vic Theatre School, her first acting roles were with the Royal

Shakespeare Company where she played alongside the likes of Judi Dench, Diana Rigg, Ian Richardson and Ian Holm. She had numerous TV roles over the years including Eth in the TV version of 'The Glums', Fletch's daughter in 'Porridge' and a starring role in the short-lived soap 'Eldorado'. More recently she was in East Enders, Coronation Street, Doctors, Midsummer Murders and Casualty. According to Liz Previtt she was 2 years older than she, and I, were.

In 1939 and 1950 there were 5 grocers. Apart from Webb's in Newbridge Road there was Edmund Bartlett at 6 Chelsea Road, Pennington's at no 8, the Co-op at the top (no number given) and Pratt's at no 14 (Sidney Carter in 1939). Indeed in 1961 there was a sixth grocer at **10 Chelsea Road** when **Mr W Ring** replaced the Halls Dairy shop (to be succeeded in 1963 by another grocer, **Mr RW Sliver**). I don't remember Rings, nor Silvers at no 10, nor Bartlett's at No 6, who were succeeded in 1952 by **AJ Thomas** and in 1961 by **Windett & Sons**, grocers. According to Elizabeth Previtt, Graham Windett was at Newbridge Junior School with us in the 1950s, and later went to the Methodist Youth Club. By 1969 and 1970 number 6 Chelsea Road was vacant to become by 1974 (what it is now) the site of the **Spar Supermarket**.

Pennington's and Pratt's were general provisions merchants that supplied the bulk of a household's weekly needs - after a visit to the butcher, baker, fruiterer, greengrocer and ironmonger (for batteries etc.). Pennington's were noted for their home cooked ham and pork pies, Pratt's had first rate cheese, freshly cut. They were different in many ways from the 'Open all Hours' convenience stores of later years. In those days of strict shop hours 'Open all Hours' was far from the case, and I remember in the late 1970s when my wife had to knock up a less than pleased Mr Pennington on Christmas Eve, after he had closed and retired to his home, when my mother had forgotten her chipolatas. Ernest Pennington's son Tony worked with him in the shop. Tony had a sister Ann, who was a schoolteacher, and an older sister, Margaret, who went to Australia for a while.

The Co-op at the top of Chelsea Road was established by 1939. It was like an old style Sainsbury shop with counters either side linked to an enclosed cash desk in the middle by an overhead wire for shooting payments and receipts back and forth. At the grocers sugar and dried fruit was weighed up into sturdy paper bags, cheese bacon and ham was sliced up at the counter. The arrival of the Spar supermarket in the 1970s did for the old Co-op from which my mother's weekly groceries orders were delivered on a bike with box holder on the front. The Co-op, similar in style to one on Combe Down, is now The Chelsea Café. My mother and my friend Philip Russell's mother met at the Co-op shortly before we started school. The Co-op Movement was more than a shop with 'divi' (although they had a large department store in Westgate Street to rival Colmers, Evans and Owens and Jolly's) – it was a social and political force with a women's guild, youth clubs and a political party affiliated to the Labour Party with its own Sunday paper 'Reynolds News' that my father read.

In 1939 and 1950 there was a second fishmonger in the road - Osborne's at **7 Chelsea Road**: this may have been the same person or a relative of the George Osborne who lived at 14 Chelsea Road in 1901. By 1955 EM Vote was established as the fishmonger at this address. *I recollect Richard Vote at school with me at CBBS (1958-65) and so I guess Votes sold fish at no 7 until late 1950s, early 1960s.* Certainly in 1961 the shop was Robbies, fishmongers. This shop was in 1968 and 1969 Sumsion Greengrocers but by 1970, and after 1974, it was Parkside Greengrocers - presumably competing with the energetic Gane's family and Mrs Wise at no 13. It is now Justin Hunter, Estate Agent.

The numbering of Chelsea Road after 7 and before 9 has been a bit obscure (or rather non-existent) in the past. Curiously the 1895 Post Office Directory precisely lists 1-8 Chelsea Road in the way that subsequent directories do not. The Kelly's Directory for 1937 lists Pennington's, Newman's Ironmongers and Lake, florists, but gives no numbers – although the 1939 Register does list Pennington at number 8. I understand that originally the Pennington's lived at 8 Chelsea Road with their shop to the north side of their building, initially sharing the same address. According to Tony Pennington, in 1964 his parents had a new building built to the north of their home and shop - and they moved to the new premises (and the shop which is now **8b Chelsea Road** and the location now of the Chelsea Clipper, a hairdresser). Their old house front (indeed their sitting room and front door) became another shop front - now **7a (Homecharmer)**.

The Pennington's old shop is now number 8 - part of the delicatessen which continues at number 8a. In 1981 the Penningtons sold their shop at 8b as a going concern to a couple of ladies who ran it as a delicatessen for 3 or 4 years before it then became the Chelsea Clipper as it is now. Tony Pennington had moved to Rosslyn Road in 1978 - he now lives in Castle Cary, Somerset.

The 1969, 1970 and 1974 directories list the following shops by number. Listed at **7a Chelsea Road** is the Chelsea Shoe Shop that did shoe repairs. It is currently the location of 'Homecharmer'. I am advised by Stuart James, who currently runs the shop, that it became 'Homecharmer' when, in July 1977, Brian Thomas established it as a 'paint, wallpaper and decorating' shop. He only kept it for 2 or 3 months before selling it to Bob Hamblin who introduced other DIY lines before selling the business to Stuart and Christine James who widened the shop's scope to include ironmongery and hardware. They are still currently running the business.

Next at **8 Chelsea Road** was Cavill & Son from about 1967 until after 1970, succeeded in 1974 by 'Colorwise' paint and wallpaper merchants). Subsequently, Stuart James tells me, it became a video rental shop and then a health food shop, followed by a delicatessen which was called Picnics. Sadly Louise and her husband who ran it had to close it in 2012 (here is a picture of Louise and Brian Jeffries on their last day of trading). It is now part of the Chelsea Road Delicatessen.

In 1968 and 1970 Giddings watch makers were at **8a Chelsea Road** but in 1974 it was the premises of FH Moss (Colourvision) Ltd – a television retailer competing with Sidney Burge at number 18. Martin Pratt has told me that at some stage after that it was a jewellers. Until the early 1990s the left hand premises of the current Deli (i.e. 8a) was Chelsea Sports shop run by a Dave Clements who used to play cricket for Bath when Martin Pratt played cricket for Lansdown *(at their ground near the RUH)*. It is now part of the Chelsea Road Delicatessen. For the story of the premises at 8b please see my notes on the previous page.

I remember, at what is now **8c Chelsea Road**, Newman's Ironmongers (who were listed as there in the years 1939- 1974). According to Stuart James it then became Jed's Electrical Repair Shop before becoming, as it is now, The Chelsea Road

Greengrocers. I also remember, at what is now **8d Chelsea Road**, Hardings the florists who were there in 1950 (and were probably there in 1939). In 1952 a Mrs D Collyer, Florist & Seedsman, replaced the Hardings - and was still there in 1961. However, in 1963 and 1974 as the Chelsea Flower Shop, it was run by Gill and Witty. Subsequently it became Jonquils flower shop. Stuart James has told me that it was the premises of Interior Harmony (Kitchens and Flooring) and then Global Tiles (Bobs Tiles) before becoming, as it is now, Paprika (selling fancy gifts).

The afore-mentioned Co-op was (at what is now) **8e Chelsea Road**. In 1992 I understand it was a florist before becoming what it is now The Chelsea Café.

LOOKING AROUND THE UPPER CHELSEA ROAD AREA

At the top of Chelsea Road is the New Crown Inn: one of only 3 premises in the Chelsea Road area that has retained its original function (the others being the Post Office and the bakers). As noted above it came into existence after 1878, replacing a pub called The Crown. In the 1970s it was run by a glamorous middle aged couple Arthur and Joyce Brown. I remember enjoying their Bristol Courage and real draught Worthington E (actually Bass - but that is how it was sold in Bath under an arrangement that dated back to the days of the Rhode Brewery).

In the 1970s after a brief revival, before the closure of Courage's Bristol brewery, Georges Home Brewed in bottle was available. In the small lounge bar a genial old guy called 'Pop' used to sit by the bar ready for you to buy him the odd pint. When Arthur died Joyce briefly worked at the Windsor Castle pub next to the road bridge (near what was once the gasworks). Sadly the Windsor Castle is no longer a pub. The picture below shows Joyce, Arthur, Ann White (to whom Penny James and I are indebted for this photo) and Pop.

In 1939 and in the 1950s, further down, between the Crown and the Weston Hotel at **11 Newbridge Hill**, lived Sidney Wilmot a builder (according to the 1939 Register, born 1918). He lived there with his sister (they were both unmarried) and his mother Lillian (born 1875). His sister Miss Lillian A Wilmot LTCL (born 1896) was for a time the piano teacher by whom my brother and I were taught to certain basic certificate levels and for the Mid Somerset music competition. She was a cat and dog lover, and had a dog called 'Paddy'. She was a keen supporter of the PDSA giving out copies of their flimsy magazine 'Animal Ways'. She and her brother were still there in the 1970s.

The Methodist Church in Newbridge Hill was shown on the 1903 OS map and was listed in the directory of 1914 as the 'Walcot Wesleyan Church'. It has a large hall in its basement accessed from grounds in Kennington Road. It was there that my mother obtained supplies for her family of Ministry of Food Orange Juice, malt extract and large tins of powdered milk (very useful later as storage for DIY materials). She also attended meetings of the Townswomen's Guild there. Liz Prevett (nee Baxter) and Philip Russell attended Sunday School there, as did my brother and I until my mother decided that it was too rowdy. Roger and I were then packed off on a Sunday afternoon to Emmanuel Church in Apsley Road (a sub-church of St John's on the Upper Bristol Road) to be bribed with coloured religious stickers to paste in booklets by sincere husky ladies who taught us all the key creeds and catechisms of the Church of England.

The Methodist Church Sunday School Superintendant (an Admiralty civil servant) Harold Jones lived on the north side of the road, opposite the church, at 10 Newbridge Hill. Liz Prevett still has a book which was a prize at Sunday School that was signed by him. It was in the garden of his house that in the mid 1950s my friend Phillip Russell and I joined his son Trevor Jones to bury Trevor's pet bat Billy – with due obsequies! Trevor was a contemporary of mine at Newbridge Junior School and the City of Bath Boy's School. He was born December 1946 in Sheffield but must have moved to Bath by 1950. His interest in music was reflected in the Blue Sahara Stompers Jazz Band he formed with other CBBS pupils, Dan Maddicott and Robert Orledge. Dan became a producer of children's TV programmes and Bob Orledge a renowned expert on the composer Eric Satie. Trevor has had an even more interesting career.

After CBBS Trevor Jones studied for his MA (Oxon), B.Mus., ARCM, and was a Trevelyan Scholar at Christ Church, Oxford. In 1976 he joined the staff of the London University's Music Department before becoming a full-time composer. He would then begin a 30-year working relationship with Eric Idle and the Monty Python team.

He changed his name to John Du Prez to avoid confusion with the South African film composer Trevor Jones.

John Du Prez is probably best known as the trumpet and horn player in the 1980s pop group Modern Romance, who had a string of Top 40 hits from 1981–83, and made many guest appearances on TV shows such as the BBC programme 'Top of the Pops'. He remained with them throughout their most successful years. He appeared on their debut album *Adventures in Clubland* (1981) and on two further albums: *Trick of the Light* (1983) and *Party Tonight* (1983).

As a composer John Du Prez composed the score for a number of films: Monty Python's The Meaning of Life (1983); Oxford Blues (1984); A Private Function (1984); Once Bitten (1985); A Fish Called Wanda (1988); Teenage Mutant Ninja Turtles 1-3 (1990-93); Carry On Columbus (1992); and Fascination (2004). He has also composed music for a number of TV series – most recently the current series of 'The Clangers' working with his life-time friend Dan Maddicott as Producer. He is especially noted as the composer, with his friend from college days, Eric Idle, of the musical 'Spamalot'.

Further down at **63 Newbridge Hill** was our doctor's surgery. Peter Rubery tells me it was once a school (I cannot confirm that). It was also the residence of Dr Brice, who drove a big Wolseley - but Dr Drew also practised there. By 1970 Mrs Brice still lived there but the practice was that of Doctors Drew, Powell and Lloyd.

In those days doctors called on you - and when my brother and I were recovering from measles Dr Drew asked my mother for newspapers and scissors. Concerned at this unusual turn in our treatment my mother bustled off like a mid-wife seeking hot water! Dr Drew then rolled up the papers and slit them half-way to create paper trees for our entertainment! Elizabeth Previtt (nee Baxter) remembers Dr Drew visiting her with a budgies egg in his case, which he showed to her. He and his family lived at 52 Combe Park. In 1973 he wrote a very chatty letter of family news to my mother on accepting into his care my father's Aunt Annie, who had come to live with my parents in Foxcombe Road.

Locksbrook Cemetery is a great tract of land north of Chelsea Road, sandwiched between Combe Park, Cedric Road, Newbridge Hill and Hungerford Road, and with the Locks Brook running through it. Locksbrook Cemetery is an unknown territory to most local people. It is a municipal cemetery that was opened in 1864 as Walcot Cemetery to serve the parishes of Walcot, Weston and St Saviours. It was consecrated on 27 September 1877 by the Bishop of Bath and Wells and administered by a burial board with sections for Anglicans and nonconformists. The press report on the consecration said that the burial board "have been able to effect an arrangement with the representatives of the parishes of Walcot and St. Saviour's, for the use of the present chapel for all interments from Weston, thus saving to the latter place the expense of providing an extra building of the kind."

The same report continues "One seventh of the entire ground is appropriated for the burial of Dissenters, and another strip is set apart for St. Saviour's, in consideration of some portion of the land being used in the construction of new roads." It closed in 1937 together with St James Cemetery (on the Lower Bristol Road) when Haycombe Cemetery was opened. There have been over 30,000 burials there. The number of the great and good, famous and less famous, which are here buried, is comparable to those in the Abbey or Lansdown Cemeteries. Locksbrook has a many large memorials, including a bronze sarcophagus with an angel by Edward Onslow Ford.

Some 122 of the cemetery's military graves are the responsibility of the Commonwealth War Graves Commission. 90 are from the First World War, 44 forming a war graves plot (mainly hospital deaths from the nearby Bath War Hospital), and 32 are Second World War graves that are dispersed around the cemetery. The Cemetery is designated a Nature Conservation Site in the Bath Local Plan. It is important as an area beneficial to local flora and fauna because it is not heavily used by the public, no pesticides are used in its maintenance, and it is a green oasis in an urban landscape.

Major Local Employers

By the mid 1950s Chelsea Road benefitted from the existence of various employers in the area. Not only did workers from Horstmann's Newbridge Works spill into Chelsea Road from Park Road at the end of a shift - so did workers from the hospitals and Chivers Bookbinders in the Combe Park area.

Before the NHS was set up the Royal United Hospital (RUH) was a 'voluntary hospital' reliant on charitable donations that started drying up after the Great War. A Hospital Box Scheme was established in the 1920s to help fund the RUH with money collected in boxes kept in homes throughout Bath, Somerset and Wiltshire. By the 1930s its counterpart on Combe Down was St Martin's - which was a municipal (council-run) hospital that had evolved from the old workhouse. The RUH relocated from the centre of Bath to the new hospital in Combe Park in 1932. Key players in that RUH story included my grandfather Frank Pine (who, as Chairman of the Bath Council of Friendly Societies pioneered the Bath Hospital Box Scheme in the 1920s and 1930s that saved the RUH from debt) and Cedric Chivers who promoted plans for its removal to Combe Park. They often shared the same public platforms.

CEDRIC CHIVERS (AND PERHAPS THE GREATEST BATHONIAN OF THE 20TH CENTURY)

Cedric Chivers, who lived at 9 Combe Park, was a great supporter of the Bath Hospital Box Scheme. He helped set up local committees for the scheme by arranging meetings with ward councillors and personally attending some ward meetings. He chaired a public meeting to give the scheme a good start and held an annual Guildhall reception for the scheme's workers. Later he also set in hand an appeal to raise funds to build a new hospital for the RUH in Combe Park - an exercise which his successor Aubrey Bateman carried forward with some vigour.

Chivers set up his bookbinding firm in Bath in the 1870s with its works at Portway, 64 Combe Park, behind the façade of a rustic cottage (that became integrated into the works after 1931). The works, pictured here in 1984, were located behind the cricket pavilion and cricket field next to the Royal United Hospital and, on the other side, next to The Homestead.

Chivers patented a new system of hand over-sewing of old books in 1904 and developed a transparent vellum to ensure that the decorative covers of old books could still be seen after restoration. He opened operations in New York City, and by 1908 his American operation had served up to five hundred libraries in the United States. However oversewn bindings are also often very tightly bound, so it is difficult for books' spines to open fully and lie flat. From a conservation standpoint, a primary concern about oversewing is that it is essentially irreversible. By 1986, most librarians and conservators had agreed that the threats of oversewn bindings outweighed their benefits. Now various types of adhesive bindings, especially double-fan adhesive, are favoured by library binders. Even Cedric Chivers admitted, in 1925, his methods were the best which at that time could be contrived, but allowed that there were complaints about the durability of some of his bindings as pages broke away from the sewing.

In its heyday, more than 300 people were employed at Portway in Combe Park but the company went into liquidation in 2004. Trowbridge-based Cromwell Press bought the assets of bookbinders Cedric Chivers in 2004 after it went into liquidation.

Cromwell set up Chivers Bookbinders to offer antique book restoration, paper conservation and journal binding, capitalising on the name of Cedric Chivers. Cromwell - which itself was saved from closure by Limpley Stoke businessman John Boden in January 2009 - also went into liquidation in 2010 with the loss of 40 jobs. Before being bought by Cromwell, Chivers had been based at Pucklechurch near Bristol.

Cedric Chivers was a Liberal, a good employer and a great philanthropist. He pioneered the Bath Trades Council with the trades unions and helped found the Bath Cabinet Makers as a worker's co-operative. He was the key figure in the establishment of Bath Public Library and donated many books to the library. Six of his leading cover designers were female. He was mayor of Bath six times between 1922 and his death in 1929. A widower, he chose as his Mayoress Madame Sarah Grand, a major feminist writer and campaigner in the late 19th and early 20th century (they are pictured here in the mid 1920s).

Sarah Grand played a major role in the life of the city speaking in support of many causes, including the Hospital Box Scheme and others that were quite controversial (such as aid to starving German ex-servicemen).

After Chivers death in 1929 his friend George Bernard Shaw sent a tribute. His successor Aubrey Bateman described Chivers as the greatest Bathonian in living memory. Bateman himself served as mayor 5 times in the 1930s and 1940s (in which period he was also President of the RUH). They were two very great 'hands-on' mayors.

A TRIP DOWN THE WEST SIDE OF CHELSEA ROAD: KENNINGTON ROAD AND PARK ROAD

Across the top of Chelsea Road, next to the Methodist Church and down some steps, is what I remember as a sweet shop called **'The Chalet'**. In 1950 Mrs Murray was the confectioner and in 1963 it was Mrs Ealand (in 1970 and 1974 it seemed to be disused). Previously it had been a Bath Tramways shelter, ticket and parcel office. Now it is incorporated into a bike shop at **9 Chelsea Road**: premises which had once been a fish shop. In 1895 it was the premises of George R Read, draper (by 1911 he was at 15 Chelsea Road). In 1911 and 1914 it was occupied by Powell & Smith, fishmongers and poulterers. It was Edwards Fish Shop from the First War until the 1950s - and then Battersbury, Fishmonger, in 1970, and Swifts Fishery in 1974. Martin Pratt has told me that it then continued as a fish shop run by Ron Coles who went to Weston Village. It then became a bathroom shop before becoming an antique shop. According to Stuart James the antiques shop was combined with, downstairs, a soft furnishing and upholsterers - before ending up as the Cadence Bike Shop.

Elizabeth Prevett (nee Baxter) says her father used to see "Fishy Edwards" early in the morning riding his bike to the station to collect fresh fish. Her mum asked her to get some yellow haddock one time, and he asked her if she wanted fresh. She said yes, and he picked up the white - she told him she wanted yellow but still fresh please. They started selling meat, but her mother would not buy it in case it tasted or smelt of fish. Elizabeth has told me that there was a wall in the churchyard which had a brick missing, so you could look into the toilet of the shop. Apparently some children she knew spent ages waiting there to pull the flush for him!

Kennington Road

On the way down Chelsea Road we cross Kennington Road where Elizabeth Baxter (now Prevett) lived at **4 Kennington Road**. Her father was a bus inspector and they were good friends of my parents. Here they are pictured their later years. I am pleased that several years ago Liz took us to see her mother Mrs Baxter at her retirement home in in Crowborough, Sussex, before she died.

Elizabeth's mother, Lilian Kemp, was born in 1909 in Plymouth and died aged 98 in 2008.

She met Henry Baxter (born in 1913 in Custom House, West Ham) in Plymouth when he was stationed there with the Suffolk Regiment in the mid 1930s. In 1939 Lilian was sent to Horstmanns in Bath to work in the gauge factory. After being bombed out of 2 lodgings (in Whiteway and Avondale Road) she went to live with Mr and Mrs Perry at 7 Foxcombe Road.

Lilian and Henry were married in 1942 in Dunwich, Suffolk and she lived in Foxcombe Road until the end of the War, when she and Henry moved to Oxford. When Elizabeth was expected, they returned to stay with the Perrys, and Henry joined the "Bath Tramways" as a bus conductor, until 1952/3 when they moved to 4 Kennington Road. They lived there until they moved to Sussex, near Elizabeth, in 1987.

Henry Baxter's father was wounded in the First World War, and met and married a nurse who had cared for him. She came from Dunwich in Suffolk, and when they married, they moved there. In 1932 Henry joined the Suffolk Regiment. He left the Army in the spring of 1939, but in the August was recalled for basic training. He was then in the Army then until the end of the War! He was at Dunkirk, and was on the beach for three days before getting home in the hold of an oil tanker. When they were on the beach there were air drops of food. He brought a tin of corned beef home, which was in Elizabeth's Gran's larder at Dunwich until, in the 1990s, they sent it to the Imperial War Museum. Henry also went over to France for D Day.

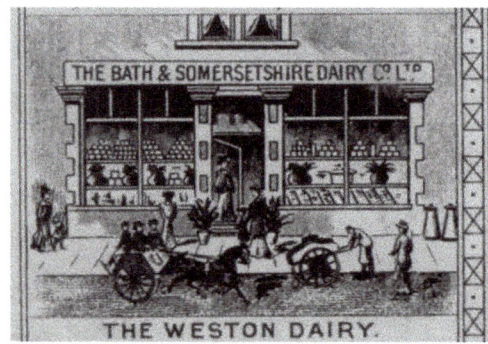 

From at least 1895 until after 1919 at **1 Kennington Road** was a branch of the Bath & Somerset Dairy Co Ltd - the company which my grandfather Frank Pine briefly ran in the early 1920s until the Norton St Philip Dairies took it over and made him redundant. The picture on the left above is from an elaborate piece of stationery used by the dairy in 1920 (for a reference for Frank Pine) and compares well with my photograph of these premises in 2018. Incidentally there was in 2018 a shop front in Junction Road, Oldfield Park with an elaborate Norton St Philip Dairies sign (pictured on the right above).

In 1922 and 1923 Kelly's listed 1 Kennington Road as a branch of the Wilts & Somerset Farmers Ltd. I suspect that Norton Dairies and Wiltshire Farmers may have been taken over by Hornby Dairies of Bristol by the 1930s.

The conscription of men and horses in the Great War greatly affected milk deliveries, despite a new female workforce, and people were encouraged to collect their milk from the local premises of the dairy - the Bath and Somerset Dairy Co Ltd had 11 such branches in the early 1920s. However there was a steady amalgamation of dairy companies from the 1920s. These dairies were all part of United Dairies by the early 1950s although street deliveries were still made under the name of Norton Dairies (albeit sometimes with Hornby Dairies vans). The growth of large dairy companies delivering from large central depots and bottling plants undoubtedly led to the sell-off of local dairy outlets.

The dairy at 1 Kennington Road was one of the outlets that was sold off. On 29 July 1922 it was sold to John Walters according to documents shown to me by his grand-daughter Helen Litherland (nee Walters). So the 1927 Kelly's listed John Walters as the dairyman at 1 Kennington Road. He came from Kelston, and from the start provided an outlet for milk from Padfield's farm in Kelston.

Born in 1876 John Walters died on 20 April 1949, at which point his son Gordon Douglas Blake Walters (born in 1910 and a RAF rear gunner in the Second World War) gave up his work with an engineering firm in Bristol to run the dairy. It was very much a family concern – with his wife Margaret Ruth Waters and children Sally, Helen and Nigel all having to lend a hand. Helen tells me that when her father said it was time to do the milk round her younger brother was always the last to scarper and hide in their rambling house with its many hidey holes. But she and Sally had to live with the guilt afterwards!

I have also spoken with Peter Rubery (who used to work for Walters Dairy). He was married to Caroline (nee Padfield) who died in 2017. She was the sister of Graham Padfield who was in my class at Newbridge Junior School. Peter has told me he used to go to Padfield's Park Farm in Kelston to collect milk, and to Paul Brunt's farm in Weston for Channel Islands milk. Walters Dairy pasteurised and bottled the milk but sometimes augmented supplies with Norton Dairies milk.

Of the pictures below, the first is a picture from Elizabeth Previtt's collection of Kennington Road c.1910 - the dairy would have been directly behind the man to the left of the picture. The second is of John Waters delivering milk by a handcart in the 1920s when milk would have been ladled out of churns into customer's jugs. By the 1930s milk was being delivered in bottles (see the third photograph below - the identity of the little girl is unknown). There are further pictures of Gordon and Peter Rubery delivering milk in the snows of 1962 and one of Helen with her parents in 1968. I am indebted to Helen for these photographs. As she has made clear to me it was hard work - cleaning equipment, collecting the milk, lifting heavy milk churns, cleaning bottles and delivering milk. Gordon invested in new bottling equipment but much of the work was labour intensive: with the individual filling of bottles and the putting on of embossed foil caps.

Walters Dairy's shop sold eggs (kept in a bowl on the counter) and dairy produce (from a single fridge - with cream ladled into wax tubs). It was run by a Miss Gibbs who managed customers' accounts. Miss Gibbs' brother was in partnership, as a builder, with George Grace, who owned the ironmongers at 11 Chelsea Road. My contemporary at Newbridge Junior School, Graham Padfield, took over running the family farm and went into cheese making. He set up the Bath Soft Cheese Company making a range of soft and hard cheeses including Bath Soft Cheese, Wyfe of Bath (a Gouda type cheese that I have much enjoyed) and the 2014 World Champion Bath Blue Cheese.

In 1971 Gordon Walters sold the dairy to a Mr Bond who ran it under the Walters Dairy name for a few years (It was listed as Walters Dairy in the 1974 Kelly's). From the summer of 2005 until March 2018, the premises at 1 Kennington Road were occupied by CG Westminster Insurance. According to Kirsty Pristo (their Agency Manager for Bath and Bristol) the premises were previously owned by someone called Kambiz - which could have been the Bath restaurant owner Kambiz Shayegan who established the Raphael Restaurant in the Upper Borough Walls in 2001 and who has also owned The Oven Pizzeria at 4 Saw Close. It is currently owned by a company called Campaero.

Next door **2 Kennington Road**, from 1914 until after 1922, was used by Charles Hale - a builder and decorator. In 1932 it was the premises of Miss LA Vincent, Hairdresser and in 1950 it was occupied by Fletcher, Ladies Hairdresser and in 1963 by Eileen, another ladies hairdresser. In the late 1950s and early 1960s Elizabeth Prevett tells me it was owned by a Mr Mortimer, who had a daughter Pat a couple of years older than her (Elizabeth's parents kept in touch with them after they moved away). In 1970 it was the premises of Beauty Box, also a hairdresser (see the adjoining picture) which, according to the Transitions Report (see table page 117), was still trading in 2012.

Currently, although rather temporary looking, the Beauty Box building can still be seen, but it is not a business premises.

In 1895 at **10 Chelsea Road** was the shop of Pickwick & Ings, grocers (any relation to Ings the grocers on Combe Down in the 1950s?). From around 1911 until well into the late 1950s it was the dairy of William J Hall. I do not know how long after 1957 Hall's Dairy survived. Nor do I know how they sourced their milk but I recollect that they had a bottling operation at the back of their premises that could be seen at the top of a lane behind this part of Chelsea Road. They used old style wide top milk bottles with a wax card disc inserted into a groove inside the top of the bottle. I am indebted to Mark Frank John Wilson for the adjoining photograph of Halls and Walters dairies' milk bottles.

In 1961 number 10 Chelsea Road was occupied by W Ring, a grocer, to be succeeded in 1963 by another grocer, R W Silver, followed by SW Hall trading as a grocer in 1965 - but in 1970 it was the Nell Gwyn, Restaurant. According to Martin Pratt, from about 1975 it had been Jo's Fish and Chip shop run by Jo and Marina Barker. Penny James has told me that when they arrived at The New Crown the Desh Restaurant had just opened in 1991/2. More recently, since May 2017, the Mai Thai restaurant has occupied these premises (according to the Bath Chronicle - this was after closure of its restaurant at 5 Pierrepoint Street in January 2017).

11 Chelsea Road was in 1895 occupied by G Hayter, greengrocer. Subsequently he moved to 13 Chelsea Road, swapping shops with the the Scudamores. William J Scudamore and then his son also called William - both ironmongers and gas fitters - were the occupiers from at least 1901 until 1950 and probably later. I do remember Mrs Grace who was the ironmonger at this address from about 1952 until at least 1970 – we used to go to her for Esso Blue for a stove that kept our downstairs (outdoor) toilet from freezing in the winter. I also remember getting an accumulator (battery) charged for an old valve radio. The shop had wooden floors and a permanent smell of paraffin. Elizabeth Previtt tells me that she had two children - she was at school with Susan, a year older than us, and Tony who was quite a bit older. Once they did not have what Elizabeth's mum had sent her for, so she bought an egg cup instead! In 1974 it was Clare's Hardware. Fairly recently it was Stacey's TV and Video Sales - but in February 2018 the shop was up for sale.

For many years **12 Chelsea Road** was a butcher's shop (and one of 3 butchers in the road). In 1895 it was run by Mrs E M Chislett. From 1911 until after 1922 the proprietor was George Mercer. Then from before 1932 until around 1970 it was the Co-op butchers. Living above the shop in 1939 was butcher Dennis J Potter and his wife.

Elizabeth Previtt tells me that in the early 1960s a Mr May was the manager and that he had three children younger than her, the eldest was Nigel. Bridget Johnston (nee Matthews) remembers them delivering meat to her parents in Audley Grove by bike with a basket on the front. In recent times these premises have been No 12 Hair Studio.

Number **13 Chelsea Road** in 1895 was occupied by W, J Scudamore, gasfitter, who subsequently swapped premises with George Hayter the greengrocer. Mr Hayter was there from about 1901 until after 1914 and then it was occupied by by the Shorney family – in 1919 and 1922 as a greengrocer, and by 1932 as a grocers. In 1939 and 1950 it was a greengrocer again - managed by Sidney Watts. He was still there in 1957 but listed as a fruiterer. From around 1961 until at least 1970 Mrs Wise was running it as a fruiterer and then as a greengrocer in competition with the Ganes family down the road!

No business was listed there in 1974. However in 1999 it was the Balti House. More recently it was Patsy's Second Hand Furniture Shop and then Armstrong & North Opticians, followed by Velopost bicycle delivery service, a bicycle delivery service in Bristol and Bath. With a head office in Radstock, Chelsea Road is its Bath delivery office.

14 Chelsea Road In 1919 and 1922 was a grocers run by George Herbert Pickwick. In 1932 and 1927, it was still a grocer's shop with JH Hiskins the proprietor. The 1939 register shows Sidney H Carter, Grocery & Provisions Shop Manager, and his family were living there. However by 1950 (indeed from the late 1940s) and for the next 50 years the grocer was Pratt's (my wife and daughter remember visiting it in the late 1980s).

Martin Pratt took over the business from his father and uncle until 1999 when he closed the grocery business because he faced the choice of being a specialist delicatessen or having to be an 'open all hours' convenience store. Whilst still living above the shop he has since leased it to other businesses: it is now Sam's Barbers Shop.

Below is a picture of the shop in the1960s. Next to it is a picture of Martin and Sandy Pratt on their last day of trading in 1999 (sadly Sandy died in January 2016).

In 1895 the corner shop at **15 Chelsea Road** was a fishmongers run by Henry Smith. From around 1901 until after 1914 it was a drapers shop run by George Read (in 1895, as noted above, he was at 9 Chelsea Road). For many years - from at least 1919 until at least 1950 and beyond - it was a drapers shop run by Miss Beatrice Williams. In 1957 Mrs Bull was the draper there followed in 1961 by a Mrs Hawkins and in 1967 by a Mrs Travell.

The premises appear to have been vacant in 1970 and 1974. In the late 1970s I believe it was a conventional café called The Chelsea Bun. It was then an Indian Restaurant and take-away. However since 1989 it has been Pizzarella run by Tony and Joan Puma. It is interesting to note that from around 1952 until after 1957 Sydney Burge, Electrical Engineer was listed at 15A before he established his shop at number 18 in the early 1960s.

Park Road

Before concluding our trip down the west side of Chelsea Road I will mention **Park Road.** In 1911 and 1914 Hooper Albert Ed, Newsagent traded at **1 Park Road**. Subsequently, in 1932, at 1 Park Road lived a William Asher, plumber (presumably with his wife Evelyn). In 1939, aged 40, he was still a plumber but his wife Evelyn (aged 34) was a shopkeeper (tobacconist, confectioner and library). In 1950 he is listed as the shopkeeper, but in 1970 it was his widow's (Mrs Asher's) sweet shop. On Thursday afternoon half days my Aunts Phyllis and Edna visited us in Foxcombe Road with our comics (Eagle, Lion and Childrens Newspaper) and pocket money. My brother and I often spent our money at Mrs Ashers. I found Cadbury's Dairy Milk too bland and sweet and I preferred what their sister company (since 1919) Fry's made at their local factory. I enjoyed Fry's Five Boys and the other Fry's brands like Tiffin, Picnic, and Crunchie (now branded Cadbury's). Fry's branded chocolate still comes in the form of Turkish Delight and Chocolate Cream (arguably the world's oldest chocolate bar). Sadly Fry's of Somerdale, near Keynsham, closed after the take-over by Kraft-Mondalez, despite promises to keep it open.

1 Park Road is currently Schmidt's Kitchens and Bathroom Solutions. Living at **10 Park Road** in the 1950s and 1960s was the Lynn family – Bill Lynn was a contemporary of my brother at Newbridge Junior School and CBBS.

So we go to the southern corner of Park Road – **16 Chelsea Road** – that was for years an off licence. In 1901 William Dutch was a grocer, wine and sprit merchant there. In 1911 and 1914 a Mr Tressider ran it as a grocer. However, in 1919, Mrs Henrietta Thorley was listed as a Beer Merchant at this address. In 1922 the premises were listed as 'Bath Brewery Ltd, Thorley Mrs.' and in 1932 'Thorley Mrs, Wine & Sprit Merchant'. In 1939 Frederick Phillips was the licensee of the off licence. In 1950 it was the premises of 'Frdk R Phillips, Wine Merchant' and in 1961-3 a Mrs L M Hibbs was the wine merchant. By 1965 until after 1974 it was 'Arthur Cooper Ltd, Wines & Spirits' (I believe a subsidiary of Courage's Brewery).

By 1999 it was Threshers (as pictured here) but in 2009 the chain went into liquidation and the shops were shut. For a couple of years it was then a florist, 'Flowers of Perfection'.

Since 2013 it has been a charity shop: HUGS - Help Us Give Support (for the RUH). My grandfather Frank Pine, who was instrumental in the inter-war RUH hospital box scheme, would have been interested in the RUH depending on this charity.

As mentioned previously - **17 Chelsea Road** was Eastmans Ltd, Butcher, from at least 1911 until 1963 and later. At some stage it was The Chelsea Road Fruit and Veg Store (from a sign recently exposed by building works). By 1967 it had become Speedamatic, Self Service Laundry which it remained for over 50 years. However, following the death of the husband of its owner Vera Podger, in February 2018 it was undertaking renovations and with a view its sale or rental as a conventional shop. On 3 December 2018 Nash & Co, estate agents, opened at 17 Chelsea Road where the launderette had been. Duncan Nash, the Director of the company, previously worked at Palmer Snell in Chelsea Road.

Number **18 Chelsea Road** was from at least 1911 until after 1950 Brooks Dye Works Ltd. By 1961 it was the shop of Sidney Burge, Radio & TV Engineer and then by 1985 it was Nixey and Smith's electrical shop. In 1992 it was Palmer Snell, Estate and Letting Agents. It is now Beyond Beauty, a beauty parlour.

The last shop on this side actually has had an address in Newbridge Road. From at least 1895 (when houses in Newbridge Road had no numbers) premises called 'Fairview' - which by 1911 had become 112 Newbridge Road - was (until after 1927) William Loveless's Chemist Shop. In 1932 and until at least 1963 it was Luther Wilson's Chemists (renumbered as **22 Newbridge Road** in the mid 1930s). Elizabeth Prevett recollects that every Sunday afternoon Mrs Wilson cleaned the dispensary. It is now Newbridgestore, a convenience store competing with Spar, using the address of **20 Chelsea Road.**

SCHOOL DAYS (AND A BIT OF INDUSTRIAL ARCHAEOLOGY)

Weston St John's Infant School

In 1952, when my family was living at 17 Foxcombe Road and I was 5, I went to Weston St John's Infant School (pictured here) where I met my life-long friend Philip Russell, who lived at 61 Hungerford Road. His father was a printer and his grandfather Reg, who lived with them, played in a London orchestra until deafness ended his career. At 46 Hungerford Road lived another friend John Kennard, whose father was the caretaker of the brand new Newbridge Junior School. In our first infant's year at Weston St John's School, in order to accommodate our 'bulge year', we were accommodated in prefabricated huts on Victoria Park Common (now part of the children's play area). However in our second year we ended up in the Victorian buildings of the infant school, before transferring to Newbridge Junior School in 1954.

The Victorian Weston St John's Infant School faced onto the Upper Bristol Road, at the junction with Locksbrook Road (the building is still there - see the above picture). Two of the teachers were Miss Sparks and Mrs Boyle. Miss Sparks made Elizabeth Baxter sit eating cold mashed potato, which she had refused to eat at lunch, when everyone else was out in the playground. Miss Carter was the favourite teacher of Jane Brimble (nee Fudge). On the opposite side of the road was, to the west, the entrance to Locksbrook Cemetery and, to the east, Turvey and Sons the stonemasons (there is still a mason's premises there). Weston St John's closed when the primary departments at Newbridge expanded in the 1970s.

Across Locksbrook Road junction is a building that is now a grocery store and café (see picture here).

The lane alongside it leads to the remains of a field that, in my younger days, was sometimes visited by the farmer with a cart pulled by 2 shire horses. My friends Philip and Elizabeth remember him too. I remember him as Farmer Weston, with a farm some way away, but independently they remembered him as Mr Kelston - curiously yet another name of local geography. Although he might have relished the link to more rural areas, as something of a self-styled traditional farmer - he may never have been more than a smallholder and his surname appears to have been Kelson. But let's not forget that by the 1960s Adge Cutler and the Worzels were celebrating a kind of nostalgia for a rural life that a Victorian generation had sought to escape.

Philip Russell has commented that he remembered him as a man out of time, even in the 1950s. The 1922, 1932 and 1950 Post Office Directories and the 1971/2 Kelly's list William Kelson as living at 8 Windsor Villas backing onto his field. The 1922 and 1932 Directories list William J Kelson as a haulier. The 1939 Register lists him as a dairy farmer and horse haulier - he is shown (born 1898) living with his sisters Violet (born 1896) and Ivy (born 1899) and they are all single. Delving back into the census data - in 1901 and 1911 he is living at 8 Windsor Villas with his family - his father, also William, is recorded as a licensed Victualler (in 1902 a James Kelson was the landlord at the Windsor Castle). I cannot find a record of his death.

Farmer Kelson's two white horses were kept in the field at Locksbrook, at least part of the time. Philip tells me they were called John and Jane. He was always a bit puzzled as to what he actually did (as he surely couldn't really have farmed, or at least not at that time, in Lower Weston) but he always used to be going about his business with the cart and horses. Philip says that, if his memory serves, one winter when the Avon was in spate one of the horses fell into the river and drowned.

A friend of Elizabeth Previtt, Neil Garrett (who used to live in Locksbrook Road), has told her that he remembered him well: "We used to ride on the cart to cut the hay in

Locksbrook Cemetery and then back to his field to build a haystack. A big man he used to wear collarless shirts, a big belt to keep his belly up and leather gaiters. He was a typical old fashioned farmer. His sister was a funny little woman, who always wore a light brown overall coat. He lived in Windsor Place *(actually as noted above – it was Windsor Villas opposite)* with his sister, neither married. His farm buildings were near the Windsor Castle Inn now all re-developed."

Bridget Johnston (formerly Matthews, then Martland) has said to me: "All I remember is Farmer Kelson had a small holding at the side of the Windsor Castle (flats are there now). He kept chicken and cows on his field by the river along with the 2 Shire horses that he walked from the stables on his land to the field where Gainsborough Gardens is now. It was then the grounds of Brookfield House, which was pulled down in the 1960s to build Gainsborough Gardens. Each morning he would bring the horses along Blackberry Lane (now Audley Park Road) down Edward Street and eventually cross the main road to the stables. He would fix an open trap to the horses and go all around the various parks in Bath collecting the grass cuttings on behalf of Bath City Council. In the evening he took the horses back to the field. He would always give us children a ride on the backs of the horses, 2 on each as I remember. They were huge and white. When you were lifted off not only did you smell of horse but you were covered in white hair! Fancy that happening now! Old Edward Street was always a challenge as it was very steep."

A little further east, on the north side of the Upper Bristol Road was the entrance to Hungerford Road followed by Mrs Porch's butcher's shop (now Clarkson's Independent Funeral Service). Next, opposite the Windsor Castle pub, there was the Police Station and Weston Magistrates Court (pictured above being pulled down in April 1961). This was then the site for a garage - but it is now a TESCO convenience store built in a style much more in line with the previous police station and magistrates court (as shown in the second picture above).

On the same side as the Windsor castle was a footpath to a footbridge and then the gasworks. Although then part of a nationalised industry, in the days before natural gas 'town gas' was still made from coal in a process that also produced coke. Coke wagons were shunted on tracks around the gasometers by two tank engines, one of which was made by Pecketts of Bristol. The tracks linked to the Midland main line. Between the gasworks and the Bath Green Park train sheds was the Stothert & Pitt Works. Peter Rubery remembers coal also being brought to the gasworks by barge.

Further on along the north side of the Upper Bristol Road towards the park - next to a chip shop (recently an Indian take-away 'Curry Nights' it is now vacant) and opposite the gasworks - was the rather plain St John's Church (pictured c1900). It has a ceiling like a collection of a child's coloured play bricks.

This is where my secondary school colleague Christopher Morgan's father was the vicar. His father was an army chaplain in Norway during the war and I think Christopher's mother was Norwegian. The vicarage (or 'Homestead') was in Combe Park. It has now disappeared in a substantial redevelopment. Christopher retired from the post of the Bishop of Colchester in 2013.

In a book 'Rambles about Bath' published in 1889 there is a passage that refers to "the Church of St. John the Evangelist, erected as a Chapel-of-Ease to the Parish Church of Weston, but now the Church of a district formed from Lower Weston." So originally it was a daughter church of All Saints Weston Village, much as Emmanuel Church in Apsley Road is now to St John's. The same book also notes "Behind lies St. Michael's Cemetery, consisting of about two acres" - it is a cemetery that is now as much a mystery to many residents as Locksbrook Cemetery.

Continuing further along the Upper Bristol Road, after a row of houses and shops, is the Royal Victoria Park where I attended infant's school in my first year of schooling. As noted above, to house my post-war 'bulge' year several prefabricated classrooms were built on the west side of the Lower Common.

In my second year my route to the Victorian buildings of the infant school was not along the main road but down Station Road, along Ashley Avenue and then passing the front of Weston Railway Station to go along a lane to the school's playground entrance. There were tin huts for toilets in the playground. My mother, Mrs Baxter and Mrs Tobin took turns to walk us to and from school.

Newbridge Junior School

For my route to Newbridge Junior School (pictured here c.1960) I had two choices. One way was to head along Kennington Road and up Chelsea Road and along Newbridge Hill, crossing over Rosslyn Road. You then entered the school grounds by a gate next to the barn at the top of the playing field (where Mr Hanff had his art classes) - on the other side, to the west at 117 Newbridge Hill, was the Council's children's home. You then went down a public path to Charmouth Road, alongside the school's playing field. The alternative was along Park Road and south out of Chelsea Road, then west along Newbridge Road, crossing Rosslyn Road before going up Charmouth Road to the school entrance. One of the children from the children's home who attended Newbridge School was someone I remember as Frankie Rowe, a valiant lad in callipers.

Newbridge Junior School was built to a standard rarely equalled since. Miss Alderwick was the headmistress (Peter Rubery remembers her as a teacher at the old St John's Junior School). Based upon a two form entry it had 8 classrooms ranked in pairs around twin central staircases. Outside each pair of classrooms there was a water fountain for drinking. Each classroom had large picture windows and a decent sized preparation room for teachers. The classrooms looked out onto an orchard (where Mr Hanff kept bees) and a grassy area. There was a good hall/gym, a library and a canteen. There were 2 kilns for pottery making (electric and fired): we made a lot of pottery with Mr Hanff. At the back there were 2 cloakrooms and toilets and 2 playgrounds (for the different ages) and a wilderness and grotto for nature study. Water fountains for drinking were readily available outdoors in a covered rear entrance and outside the cloakrooms. I have taken the liberty of appending some old school photos that show the younger selves of some that I have mentioned elsewhere in this narrative.

In our years at Newbridge Junior School Philip Russell and I were first taught by Mrs Jones and then by the reserved but charismatic and immensely creative Dietrich Hanff.

His brief biography 'Out of Nazi Germany' portrayed his arrival in the UK in 1938 as a Jewish teenager of 17 where he was effectively adopted by Robin and

Heather Tanner (here they are c.1987 - sadly all 3 died within the next 6 years). He later taught at Newton Park Teachers Training College (now the Bath Spa University).

In 1957, at the time of Ghanaian independence in March that year, Mr Hanff brought a Ghanaian family to talk to us about life, clothes, food etc. in Ghana. During the 1980s, BBC television producer Margaret Benton made a film called *Look Stranger: A Vision of Wiltshire* which was released in 1987. This documented and celebrated Heather, Robin and Dietrich Hanff's home life, creativity, beliefs and love of the Wiltshire countryside.

Three other male teachers, who did not teach me, were the aforementioned Mr Reeves, a Mr Mills and a Mr Walker (who died aged 95 in 2018). Mr Mills took pupils to Friday afternoon swimming lessons at the Beau Street Baths.

After Mr Hanff my class had Miss Tucker and finally Miss Gertrude Pointing as our class teachers (in the pre-11 plus cramming period). Miss Pointing had taught my mother at Combe Down School in the early 1920s (probably as a pupil-teacher). Gertrude Carrie Pointing was born 1 August 1901 in Corston. Although only 57 she looked quite old (as a photo Elizabeth Prevett - nee Baxter - took on a school outing in 1958 indicates). She sometimes appeared to have dozed off in quieter class work periods.

Many of us went home for lunch (I only had to cross one minor road - Rosslyn Road - to do so) and some lunchtimes Miss Pointing got one of the girls to get Rock Salmon for her cat from Fishy Edwards! Elizabeth Baxter who lived at 4 Kennington Road had this honour more than once and each time she was given a penny for her trouble. Liz was a nurse at the RUH when Miss Pointing was brought in for treatment in 1973: she said 'You are Elizabeth Baxter. You were a little devil at school'! Luckily for both of them, Liz was just going off on holiday at the time! Miss Pointing died in Corston on 1 April 1973 (aged 71).

In a parallel stream to mine John Hayden was taught by a Miss Ancrum in the first year followed by Mrs Morton in the second year, Mr Hanff in the third year and Mr Walker in the final year. My memories of Newbridge Junior School include lining the road in Newbridge Hill in 1958 for the visit of the Emperor of Ethiopia when he donated Fairfield House, Newbridge, to the city - he had lived there in exile during the war.

Leisure Time

Our leisure time from school was typical of its time. In the 1950s few people had cars - maybe 3 or 4 cars might be parked in Foxcombe Road. So quite young children might play in the road. By the age of 11 you might roam quite freely in the holidays (subject to the injunction to return for mealtimes) - perhaps to Victoria Park to be spooked by the eerie Great Dell, with its monuments to Jupiter and Shakespeare, or to sail boats on the Upper Common boating pond (sadly no more). Or else we might trespass on the derelict plot that sloped down from Edward Street to the Ashley Grove end of Hungerford Road called Beezer's site (after the builder CH Beezer who owned it).

We might go down Audley Park Road (then just a lane we called Blackberry Lane) to see the tramp who lived in the bushes. Or we might go train-spotting: perhaps trespassing on railway land near the entrance to Bath Green Park train sheds to see the exclusively S&D class of 7Fs - or to see the Pines Express driven by the legendary Donald Beale and his fireman Pete Smith (both the subject of a TV documentary in the 1980s).

Like many at that time, my father worked a 5½ day week. So when I was quite young I might go with him on a Saturday lunchtime by 3 buses (to Bath, to Chippenham, and then on to Littleton Drew) to stay overnight with my grandmother. We invariably returned Sunday evening with my Uncle Tom on his Ariel motorbike and sidecar combination. Other Saturday afternoons my father might take me and my brother to stand in a sea of cloth caps and cigarette smoke to see the legendary Stan Mortensen and local boy Tony Book play for the Southern League Bath City at Twerton Park.

The picture below, according to respondents on the Bathonian's Past and Present Facebook pages, is probably the City v Swindon FA Cup replay of 10 November 1960. Chris Stone has suggested it was played on a Thursday kicking off at 2 pm (as there were no floodlights at Twerton Park then) and he believes that some schools gave their children a half day off, which could account for the amount of school uniforms.

Also Chris has mentioned that several local companies gave their employees a half day as well so they could attend the game if they wished. So that is why I am standing on the rails with my father behind the corner flag, and my younger brother (who had just started wearing spectacles), is chewing his programme to the right of us in the picture.

City of Bath Boy's School

In 1958 I went to school at the City of Bath Boy's School. My time there and my teenage years are another story. However my journey to school when I didn't take the number 4 to The Bear Flat involved walking down Station Road and crossing Locksbook Road where, a few doors down to the west, was the **Cleverley Victor Sweetland Organ Company.** These premises are shown in the Ordnance Survey in 1902 as a Gospel Hall, and in 1932 as a Congregational Church. They are now a Church of Jesus Christ of the Latter Day Saints).

I then went across the pedestrian Half Penny Bridge over the River Avon with views to the west of Weston Island dominated by **Stothert and Pitt's** cranes. The company dated from 1785 in Bath. Sadly Stothert and Pitt as a major manufacturer has disappeared without trace (they never adapted to making container cranes and were let down by Robert Maxwell). They were the builders of a variety of engineering products ranging from dockyard cranes to construction plant and household cast iron items. They went out of business in 1989 after a management buy-out in 1988 following the collapse of the Maxwell empire. The name and intellectual property became part of Clarke Chapman.

In my journey to school I would then pass, to the west, alongside Fieldings Road, the factory of the **Bath Cabinet Makers (BCM).** Bath Cabinet Makers was founded as a worker's co-operative in 1892 and owed its existence to a strike at F and A Norris Brothers' Bath's Albion Cabinet Works in December 1891. The following year, Charles Richter, an employee at Albion, launched the Bath and West Co-operative Cabinet Makers Ltd. The intention was determinedly idealistic; men needed jobs and the city provided enterprise. Shareholders were represented by a committee of five members, one of whom was the influential Cedric Chivers from the bookbinding family. Richter was elected general manager the following month, and work began in rented accommodation.

From 1895 they had a factory in Bellotts Road (see the picture below left) and were famed for their arts and craft/art nouveau/art deco designer furniture that furnished the Cunard liners Queen Mary and Queen Elizabeth. William Morris considered that machines were responsible for bad design. As handwork was necessarily time-consuming, his furniture was too expensive for the very people he wanted to supply.

In contrast, Charles Richter, a committed socialist and natural progressive, deplored asking men to perform arduous tasks that could easily be accomplished by machine. In Bath Cabinet Makers's early days, he set up an Education Committee and ran games and dramatic clubs. Like Cedric Chivers he was acquainted with George Bernard Shaw, and he asked the playwright down to Bath for a performance of Caesar and Cleopatra.

Subsequently BCM built the factory just off the Lower Bristol Road that is illustrated above right– this is the factory that I would have passed on my walk to CBBS in the first 5 years of the 1960s. In 1959 BCM was taken over by Yatton Furniture (makers of Avalon furniture). In the early 1970s the Yatton company became part of the Christie-Tyler furniture group (making Arkana furniture). In 1986 BCM was acquired by Ken Fullalove, one of their directors, in a short-lived management buy-out.

A new award-winning factory was built by BCM adjacent to their old one in 1966-67 but this was taken over in 1970 by the US furniture maker **Herman Miller**, who then built a further award winning factory on the opposite side of the river in Locksbrook Road (Wood Mill) in 1975. The former new BCM factory is now a Lidl supermarket.

The Herman Miller company have kindly supplied me with the following photos of their two Bath factories. The picture of the newly built BCM factory they took over in 1970 (with the older BCM factory in the background), and the factory they built in 1975, across the river from their other works and next to the Horstman premises (mentioned above in the section about the Horstmanns).

The former BCM factory was grade II-listed in 2007. Built in 1966-67 to designs by the architect Brian Henderson, a partner in the notable firm of Yorke, Rosenberg and Mardall (YRM), it is the first building in Britain to use Mero space frame technology, one of the first widely commercially available space grid systems invented in Germany in the 1940s. The building is also an example of the early use of neoprene in parts of its external cladding and pre-fabricated patent glazing (all of which has been retained in the new Lidl store).

In 2015 the 1975 Herman Miller factory was grade II-listed - it is considered to be an early and important example of the British high-tech movement. The US furniture-maker (based in Chicago and famous for its classics of industrial design by George Nelson, Isamu Noguchi, Charles and Ray Eames and Robert Propst) wanted a fully flexible building that reflected the avant-garde design solutions it was pioneering in the late 1960s. Herman Miller's Action Office System had revolutionised the American workplace by providing a kit with which an open plan office could be easily configured using mobile division panels.

Recently production by Herman Miller was transferred out of Bath to Melksham. Since Herman Miller moved out of Wood Mill, the building has been bought by Bath Spa University who are redeveloping it and will make it the home for their School of Art and Design. Bath may not be the industrial city it once was but it has a heritage of great industrial architecture!

The older BCM factory is no longer there - it was demolished in 1994 (not long after the above picture was taken). It is now an **M&S Food Hall** and the site of **Polamco Ltd** which, as its website proclaims, is "a world renowned Backshell, Connector, Custom solution and Interconnect accessory design and manufacturing company based in Bath". These are products that, to a layman, are a bit of a mystery.

It is good to see that precision engineering still has its place in the area. Indeed that is very much the case given that, in the time that other manufacturers were in decline there was another, with a substantial establishment and world-wide base, which was establishing itself in the area.

So I must digress, to mention **Rotork**, with its headquarters in Brassmill Lane, a designer and manufacturer of industrial flow control products encompassing valve actuators, gearboxes, control systems, instrumentation and accessories. Rotork is the market leading actuator manufacturer and flow control company that operates in any market where the flow of gases or liquids needs to be controlled. Again these are products that might mystify the layman but are crucial in the regulation of pipelines in the oil industry and water supply – to give just two examples.

The Company was established as a small engineering workshop in Bristol in the 1940s. In 1945 it was acquired by *Frenchay Products* led by Jeremy Fry. It made its first actuator in 1952. In 1957 Rotork moved to Bath. Initially they operated from Widcombe Manor, Jeremy Fry's home, with 12 staff. In 1962 Rotork moved into a new production plant in Brassmill Lane, Newbridge, Bath, which remains the company's headquarters. It was first listed on the London Stock Exchange in 1968 as Rotork Controls and is one of the UKs top 250 companies.

When Jeremy Fry lived at Widcombe Manor he hosted visits from Princess Margaret and her set. He was a scion of the chocolate family. In the 1970s Jeremy Fry was responsible for the Rotork Sea Truck (a flat-hulled, high-speed watercraft, similar to a small landing craft, made from fibreglass, they could be used to land vehicles without jetties or harbour facilities. This was designed by the design team at Smallfry led by designer Tim Fry and Anthony Smallhorn. The team had input from James Dyson whilst he was a student in the 1970s, as part of his final year's project at the Royal College of Art. Jeremy Fry was the co-designer.

On my journey to CBBS I then carried across the Lower Bristol Road. Further down that road towards Bath there was the premises of **Pitman's the printers** - another long-gone Bath firm (they closed in 2007). Their factory had/has an imposing Palladian-style frontage that the City of Bath is trying to find a use for. In the book 'Rambles about Bath' published in 1889 by Isaac Pitman there is the following passage that speaks of Pitman's and the laundry next to it towards Bath:

"Another fine building with a handsome front has been recently erected on land facing the main road just below the Church. The building is used by Messrs. Pitman and Sons for the printing of their well-known phonetic publications.

"The Sanitary Steam Laundry, built in 1882, is the property of a limited liability company, who established it with a desire to employ a large staff of workpeople who hitherto had been employed in unsanitary cottages. All the work is conducted on the most advanced and scientific principles. It is worth a visit, and those availing themselves of the free admission to the public will not fail to notice how the necessary work of washing is conducted in spacious buildings, thoroughly lighted and ventilated - at once doing away with any fear of the dangers which sanitary officers have often pointed out with respect to laundry work as ordinarily performed."

The laundry is the predecessor of the company that currently owns **Regency Cleaners** (mentioned above in relation to the premises at 1 and 2 Chelsea Road). Another progressive Bath employer to add to my list!

So, resuming my journey to school, I would then go up Inverness Road to Bellott's Road where the first BCM factory, built in 1895 used to be (see above). At Bellott's Road the former Somerset and Dorset Railway crossed over the former GWR on a steep climb out of Bath to the Devonshire and Combe Down tunnels.

Continuing via Moorland Road I would pass, opposite Woolworths, a Co-op shop over which there was a youth club that I attended. I would then go past the **Scala Cinema**, which became a Co-op Supermarket in 1962. I remember seeing the 1960 film 'Ocean's Eleven' there – it was probably an 'A' certificate film, so I would have been under-age for it! I would next carry on up King Edward's Road, Oldfield Road and Bloomfield Road to the Bear Flat and so on up to CBBS at the top of Beechen Cliff.

THE FUTURE OF CHELSEA ROAD

The Chelsea Road area has had an interesting history in the 120 or so years since it first emerged as a mainly Victorian suburb of Bath in Lower Weston. But what sort of future does it have? A significant local project and the views of a local estate agent offer some thoughts.

The Transition Project

In 2010 Transition Bath (a local voluntary environmental organisation) launched a study based on their belief that walking and cycling access to all local shopping and service areas should be encouraged and improved. Their Transport & Built Environment group had produced a map that showed that many people in Bath lived within 10 minutes' walk of a neighbourhood hub.

It was thought Chelsea Road might provide an excellent example of a neighbourhood hub where improvements might be made. This road was on the boundary of Kingsmead ward where 37% of households had no car and Newbridge ward where 25% had no car, so these residents needed to walk or cycle to the shops.

The mainly self-funded project involved:
- Background research (June 2010 – January 2011)
- Residents questionnaire on access and shopping habits (April – September 2011: total responses 689 of 2088 questionnaires, 33%)
- Residents meetings (19th March & 23rd April 2012)
- Traders survey on customer access (May 2012: total responses 24 of 35, 67%)
- Joint residents & traders meeting (Monday 2nd July 2012)
- Launch of 'Making Chelsea Road Local Centre Thrive' to present work to date to residents (Saturday 19th January 2013)
- Working group design meetings (March – April 2013)
- Survey of households on specific access proposals (July – August 2014: total responses 638 of 2301 questionnaires, 28%)
- Trader survey on specific access proposals (late 2014)
- A final public meeting at Weston Methodist Church (Friday 20th March 2015)

The 2001 national census showed a total of 2,423 households north of the river were within 10 minutes' walking distance of Chelsea Road, with 6,027 residents and a daytime population of 7,827 people. It also showed that 23% of households in the project area had no car, and 48% have only one so were likely to have limited car use within working hours. Responses to the questionnaire highlighted a number of concerns regarding Chelsea Road as it stood, as well as positive suggestions. These included:

- Amount and speed of vehicles using Chelsea Road
- Narrowness of pavements in and around Chelsea Road
- Lack of safe crossings
- Access difficulties for people with low mobility, those in wheelchairs and those with buggies
- Increased greenery and visual identity in Chelsea Road
- Opportunities for improved cycling facilities
- Potential for walking access through the cemetery, and a general call for more off-road paths

On Wednesday 2nd October 2013 (between 7am and 7pm), B&NES Council conducted a transport survey, which found that 2924 vehicles entered Chelsea Road, but only 418 stopped (about 1 in 7), 156 were already parked there, and 2506 (86%) of the vehicles passed straight through, highlighting how the road is often used as a 'rat-run'.

The unanimous decision of a design group made up of local residents was that Chelsea Road should be closed to through traffic. The impact on Kennington Road and Park Road would be monitored (as traffic would have to travel through those roads and Warwick Road to avoid a pedestrianised central sector, so allowing activity to extend into a new public space. Trees and street furniture would both improve the appearance of the street and, by interrupting views along the road, deter its use as a vehicle rat-run. There would be no net loss of parking spaces (not clear how this would be if the central section were pedestrianised) but an increase in the number of cycle racks.

The design group made various proposals and after a further survey on specific access proposals, some of the proposals in the survey had widespread support:
- having two new crossings over Newbridge Hill;
- opening up walking and cycling routes through the cemetery;
- a new bus stop on Newbridge Road.

Other elements did not get support:
- narrowing Newbridge Road at the crossing point;
- closing the central part of Chelsea Road to vehicles.

Opinion was divided over two proposals:
- moving the crossing over Newbridge Road nearer to the Post Office; and
- making the central section of Chelsea Road available for community uses (a few said the term 'community uses' was unclear).

Important concerns and comments included:
- closing part of Chelsea Road would cause worse problems on other roads;
- removing through traffic requires a left turn option or roundabout between Newbridge Road and Newbridge Hill;
- the proposals could have safety implications;
- there could be funding and value for money concerns;
- a variety of alternative traffic calming measures;
- Chelsea Road should be one way; and
- Chelsea Road should only be closed occasionally for special events.

Key Elements of the November 2012 Report

A separate questionnaire to traders was completed by 24 of the 35 distributed. Although there was no relevant question on the matter, two traders said they would like a butcher in the road and one felt the lack of a pharmacy. This reflected the shops mentioned most often in the residents questionnaires. One trader specifically said "The biggest draw for a shopping street like Chelsea Road is the mix and quality of shopping available. The quality of the shops we have is good but a wider mix would help enormously." Another said that people needed to be encouraged to shop in Chelsea Road regardless of how they got there. Fourteen traders (58%) said that "most" or "all" of their customers were local residents, and four traders (17%) said that more of their trade was from outside the local area.

Nine traders thought that "most" of their customers walked, twelve felt some did, and three considered a few came on foot. Eight traders stated that most of their customers arrived by car, while the remaining sixteen said some come this way. Only one trader felt that most of their customers arrived by cycle, nine considered some did, and fourteen said a few customers cycled. Three felt that no customers came by bus or other modes, ten said a few did, and ten thought some did and one did not answer this section.

Both residents and traders felt that the speed and level of traffic caused problems, and suggested various measures to slow speeds. They also considered that more safe crossings were needed, with both Chelsea Road itself and the roundabout at the top being mentioned as locations where crossing was difficult.

There was one major difference of priority between views of local residents and traders in relation to transport: parking. Parking in general was felt to be lacking by only one of the 689 households who responded, and one other considered that there should be more disabled parking. However, parking was the main issue of concern to the traders, mentioned by 16 (66.7%) of them.

There was remarkable agreement between householders & traders that Chelsea Road and the access routes to it would benefit from:
- Reduced speed and lower levels of traffic
- More greenery and a distinct visual identity in Chelsea Road itself
- Benches to sit on, in Chelsea Road and on access routes
- More safe crossings
- Wider pavements
- More non-road routes, especially from the east near Royal Victoria Park
- Action to tackle driving and parking on pavements
- More cycle racks and paths
- An access ramp and handrail to the Post Office and the estate agent next to it
- Solutions for those with low mobility
- A butcher, fishmonger and pharmacy
- A car club space

Parking was a more contentious issue. Only one resident of the 689 who responded considered general parking to be lacking, and another said that there was not enough space for disabled parking. Two-thirds of traders felt that more parking, not less was a priority.

Some thoughts on the Transition Report

The Transition Bath project derived from the environmental group's belief that walking and cycling access to all local shopping and service areas should be encouraged and improved. The remedies the project came up with have much to offer in terms of making Chelsea Road a safe, attractive, and environmentally friendly, place to shop - particularly for pedestrians and cyclists. The report also reported on the need for a good diversity of shops - bringing back a butcher, a pharmacy and a fish shop.

However, given its remit, the report did not address broader issues concerning the future of Chelsea Road as a shopping area. You cannot return to 1905 when pedestrians and cyclists were the only features of the road. It is not surprising that parking was the main issue of concern to the traders, mentioned by 16 (66.7%) of them. It is not insignificant that four traders (17%) said that more of their trade was from outside the local area. It is perhaps surprising that only one resident of the 689 who responded considered general parking to be lacking, given that the residential streets are choked with parked cars.

In the past Chelsea Road benefitted from the footfall of those who walked or cycled to work from employers like Horstmann, Chivers and BCM. The Locksbrook Road area is still a major industrial area of Bath but those who work there are likely to drive to work, and are unlikely to stop off in Chelsea Road to shop if parking is difficult.

Encouraging a diversity of shops is important but given the economic climate and trends in shopping that have led to the widespread closure of butchers, pharmacies and fish shops it is difficult to see how Chelsea Road could buck such trends. There are clearly no easy answers and the decline of local shopping streets is a national issue. In the 6 years since the Transition Bath report, based on a survey of 34 commercial premises, Lloyds Bank has closed, as have at 6 of the other businesses without the premises being re-occupied. What is going to fill these gaps?

Perhaps one outcome of that report is that Chelsea Road is now a 20mph Zone and a Fun Day in 2015 trialled the partial closing of the road.

Weblog of Knight Frank by Matthew Leonard June 12, 2017

For an excellent antidote to doom and gloom, one may go to an article on this weblog entitled 'Spotlight on: Newbridge and Chelsea Road' where Knight Frank's Matthew Leonard tried to explain why the Newbridge area of Bath was a thriving microcosm sometimes described as a village in itself.

He commented "The central hub of the 'village' is Chelsea Road - a vibrant hive of activity and the social focus of the area. There are a variety of excellent local shops and businesses in the road which are whole-heartedly supported by local residents like myself. The centre of Bath is either a 30 minute walk away or around 5 minutes on one of the many local buses."

He went on to say about Chelsea Road shops "We really have it all when it comes to local shops! The Newbridge area boasts a bakery, The Chelsea Road café, several hairdressers, a charity shop, dry cleaners, florists, a Hardware Store, an excellent Deli (my particular highlight), a pizza restaurant, a Spar convenience store, a greengrocer, Cadence bike shop (a meeting place for many lycra clad cyclists!)"

In terms of eating out he says "I often go out for food locally, because there's such a great choice. The recently renovated Locksbrook Inn in Newbridge does excellent food and drink and has a wonderful rear deck area overlooking the Kennet and Avon canal. It is part of the Bath Pub Company chain who also own three other Gastro Pubs in the city. The Boathouse by the river again does excellent food and has a delightful garden overlooking the water, and I also noticed recently that a micro-brewery with a "brewery tap" bar has sprung up near the canal, called the Electric Bear. It's next on my list of places to visit!"

He addresses the question of 'who lives there?' by saying "Newbridge is largely populated by young families who are attracted by the excellent primary school and the village-like nature of the area. Newbridge School is rated as 'Good' by Ofsted and is extremely popular and well thought of by all the parents that I know. Newbridge is also home to many of Bath's medical profession due to its close proximity to the Royal United Hospital and Newbridge surgery (an excellent local practice.)"

A Fun Place to Live and Shop

With such a positive approach to the area by local residents and traders its future as an area in which to live, work and play has got to be assured!

If that is not enough, then how about a bit of community spirit - and a trial run for closing part of the street! In the May 2015 there was a Chelsea Road Fun Day, as shown in the following photographs (from John Hayden).

Chelsea Road Fun Day – May 2015

CONCLUSION ON CHANGES SINCE 1950-1974
(SOME ENDINGS AND SOME NEW BEGINNINGS)

So I conclude my personal perspective of my young life in the Chelsea Road area and something of a history of the area. After Moorland Road, Oldfield Park, Chelsea Road (with 30 or more shops) was one of Bath's larger 'out of town' shopping centres. Combe Down and Weston village probably have had fewer shops.

This little work is a series of snap shots in time - as are most histories. It begins with a series of maps giving a geographical history of the area and is then based on censuses, directory records and personal memories and anecdotes. There is no such thing as a continuous record, even in this era of surveillance cameras. Inevitably great unrecorded changes can arise between those snap shots - from one record to the next. So there is every probability that things will be missed.

I have tried to explain my inspiration for this exercise and how I arrived in Foxcombe Road. I have sketched a history of the area's transport links. I have recorded some of my experiences of living in Foxcombe Road (much of which would be alien to people now). Having regard to historical maps that reveal the steady development of the area Penny James has shown how the New Crown Inn was significant in that development.

Before taking a geographical tour I have looked at the role of the Horstmann family in the area. They were not just employers, making 'Newbridge' a world-wide brand, but lived in a large number of properties in the district with an impact on local social life. It has been fascinating to discover the importance of manufacturing in the area and, through an essay by Sally Festing, the links between Cedric Chivers and the Bath Cabinet Makers - and George Bernard Shaw!

My geographical tour offers snapshots of the histories of the various premises encountered with an inevitably selective range of anecdotes and re-awakened personal memories, mainly related to the third quarter of the 20th century. I have voyaged out into the hinterland of Chelsea Road, in the north taking in Locksbrook Cemetery and two other employers (the Royal United Hospital and Cedric Chivers) and in the south I have taken in Station Road and my trips to Weston St. John's School and Newbridge Junior School.

On my trip to the City of Bath Boy's School I have looked at employers in the Locksbrook Road area. In my annexes I have appended a series of records of directories to show, in particular years, the types of shops that were then in the

Chelsea Road area. The whole exercise is inevitably far from comprehensive - I have had to be satisfied with what has been readily available to me.

Chelsea Road reflects the great changes that have occurred in our local shopping streets in the 20th century. These include the impact of the motor car, the arrival of small supermarkets, changing employment opportunities through the de-industrialisation of an area, changing spending patterns as a result of increasing affluence and the impact of the internet.

Chelsea Road's history reflects the life cycle of local neighbourhood shopping centres generally. People tend to think, at least implicitly, that village shops and local shops have always been there. But they were a creature of the late 19th early 20th century: the result of mass production and branding of packaged foods replacing markets, with the railways delivering chilled fish, fresh fruit and vegetables, milk and milk products - and also the widespread availability of dried and tinned goods. The role of the Co-operative Societies was also very significant for retailing, distribution and production, e.g. CWS, CRS and local societies (the Radstock Co-op still exists).

In the 21st century, local and neighbourhood centres have changed for reasons relating to personal mobility, concentration in the retailing industry, and of course now the Internet. However, there are positive changes, including the rise of multiple convenience stores (Sainsbury Local, Tesco Express, etc.), voluntary/symbol groups like Spar, Premier, Budgen, Nisa, Londis, Costcutter, Mace, One Stop (owned by Tesco). Leisure activities are now catered for by coffee shops, restaurants, fast food outlets and gyms. Some retailers offer internet shopping and parcel collection. In some towns ethnic food stores have also appeared.

The recent period of economic recession has led to a national concern about the decline of city centre and local shopping streets. According to a report in 'The Observer' newspaper of 18 November 2018 figures compiled by the Local Data Company showed that the number of vacant shops, pubs and restaurants in Britain rose by more than 4,400 in the first six months of 2018. The pace of decline has meant that more than one in 10 shops has lain empty. The article noted that the British Retail Consortium had reported that up to 85,000 jobs disappeared in the first nine months of the year. A huge shift in the behaviour of UK shoppers was illustrated by the fact that whilst 10 years ago 5p of every retail pound was spent on-line, experts now predicted that the figure was heading for 50p. On the other hand, whilst retail's share of overall spending was shrinking, people were opting to spend their cash on experiences such as trips to the hairdresser, beauty salon or weekends away. Chelsea Road has clearly reflected these trends.

The consequence of all these trends for Chelsea Road (with a peaking of retail representation in 1970 as shown in the table on page 106) has been the disappearance of several competing small grocers, greengrocers, butchers, sweet shops, dairies and ironmongers.

The fairly recent closure of Lloyds Bank must have been a cause of concern for local traders, not least because it attracted casual shoppers to the road. However, a craft baker has survived and so have the corner pub and the post office - somewhat against the trend. Hair dressers and barbers have remained as an essential service and there is still a greengrocer and an ironmonger. Furthermore there are now 3 cafes or restaurants, 3 home furnishings shops, 3 charity shops, 3 estate agents and several shops offering specialist services, including a beauty parlour and, (shades of the past), the depot of a bicycle delivery service. Nevertheless, in February 2018 some 6 shops were up for sale.

Some of the longer established businesses have disappeared with the demise of their ageing proprietors. If Chelsea Road was a pivot in my life, it was also a fulcrum in the wheel of fortune of the local traders - as new entrepreneurial hopes joined the carousel and older ones were sadly thrown off. As I have developed or re-established contact with those who had businesses in the road I am well aware of the joys and hopes of those establishing new businesses and the regret and sense of bereavement of those who had to close their businesses after lives of dedication and service - after trying to steer through a frequently stormy and changing economic environment. In part this book is a tribute to them: that their hopes and efforts are put on record. On the positive side Chelsea Road still has a number of innovative businesses - it has been very much a microcosm of most local shopping streets today.

De-industrialisation has had an impact on local employment opportunities in the area - with the demise of enlightened employers like Chivers' Bookbinders in Combe Park, Horstmann's, Stothert and Pitt and Bath Cabinet Makers. It is ironic that this has led to a new housing estate on the old Horstmann's site leading to an increased housing density in the area. Equally ironic is that two award winning factory sites have become a discount supermarket and a faculty of Bath Spa University. However the examples of Horstman, Polamco and Rotork mentioned above show that the traditions of industrial invention and entrepreneurship of progressive manufacturing employers (as reflected in the stories of BCM, Cedric Chivers and the Horstmann family) are still alive and kicking in the area. The Locksbrook Industrial Estate also provides a range of warehousing for retail distribution.

The area has changed in many other ways. For one thing it is rather choked with cars, although this may have led to more students living in the area. Less dependent on cars they would be attracted by the area's good bus links to the two relatively new Universities of Bath and Bath Spa and the centre of Bath. Even so more car parking for shoppers is needed.

The old throngs of workers (on foot or on bike) from Horstmann's Newbridge Works or Chivers Bookbinders are no more. They brought a lot of trade to the shops in Chelsea Road. The closure of Newbridge Works has meant that Park Road is now not only complete but has crept up Foxcombe Road. The new houses at, and above, the old Horstmann's entrance match the style of the older terrace houses - but although they have been built with parking spaces at the back they have doubtless added to the density of housing in the area and its parking problems.

The upside of an district with mainly terrace houses and on-street parking is that Chelsea Road area still has a significant hinterland for on-foot shoppers if, in this internet age (and on-line shopping), the local shops can sell what the residents want. Food outlets and florists may increasingly benefit from on-line sales. In recent times all local high streets have struggled with decay and decline. However the importance of revitalising them is still a pressing current concern - to provide a hub for local communities, and the employment, and commercial and social services they need.

PICTURES OF NEWBRIDGE JUNIOR SCHOOL FELLOW PUPILS IN THE LATE 1950s

The following pictures represent a very partial tribute to my generation who grew up in the Chelsea Road area in the 1950s and who went to Newbridge Junior School. It is a very selective set of photographs and I know that there may be in existence other photographs from that era that would include my friends, Philip Russell, Elizabeth Baxter and many others. Sadly they include people who are no longer with us like Jane Denyer, who became an artist, and David Angus, who was a school teacher.

Quite a few of those who appear in these photographs have been of assistance to me in this project on Chelsea Road – Jane Fudge, Bridget Matthews and John Hayden in particular. It was a very special school and I am grateful my grand-daughters are blessed with a similar education.

Peter Grassi; Graham Padfield; Ian Francis; Martin Chapman

John Daniels; Patricia Watts; Jane Denyer; Charlotte Flood; Cherry Wilmot; Jennifer Hughes

NEWBRIDGE JUNIOR SCHOOL 1956 MRS JONES' CLASS

Bernard Luccock
Trevor Jones
David Angus
Jane Evans, Bridget Mathews, Jane Fudge
Carolyn Derrick
Beryl White
Michael Babbage

NEWBRIDGE JUNIOR SCHOOL 1956 MRS JONES' CLASS continued

NEWBRIDGE JUNIOR SCHOOL 1957 MR HANFF'S CLASS & GHANAIANS

Julie Harris; David Angus; Andrew Greenhalgh; Miss Alderwick; Marion Reid; Roger Matthias
Vivienne Faulkner

Martin Chapman; Janet Scott; Bernard Lucock; Caroline Flood; Diane Colwell; Christine Tobin

NEWBRIDGE JUNIOR SCHOOL

Photographs from John Hayden

PICTURE ON THE LEFT c1958
John Hayden is on the right
Behind him is Michael Smith.
Nigel Crocker is on the left
Behind him is Ray Tallon,
Carolyn Derrick, Susan Parfitt .
Next to her is Brenda Harris.

PICTURE BELOW c1957
Apologies to those who have not been identified

Penny Archer   Patricia Hughes   Peter Falla   Trevor Janes
Dianne Colwell   Catherine Prentice   Nigel Crocker   Andrew Greenhalgh
                  Susan Parfitt   Peter Grassi   Glyn Warbutton

Brenda Harris / Carolyn Derrick   Arthur Dagger   John Hayden
Gillian Percival   Barry Taphouse   Martin Rogers   Graham O'Brien
                    Chris Goodman   Keith Girling   Tony Bourne   Mike Smith

LANDLORDS OF THE NEW CROWN INN

1878 John Beavis
1879 Ann Beavis
1882 Arthur Beavis
1904 William Withers
1905 Alfred Cole
1906 George Thornhill
1907 Albert Hulbert
1910 Alfred Beamish
1912 Thomas Burridge
1925 Sidney Ball
1945 Stanley Crouch
1960 Robert Cann
1965 Peter Hardy
1968 Arthur Brown
1979 William Player
1988 Nigel Amott
1990 Ben Cliffe
1992 Kelvin James

There were many changes of landlords in the early 1900s: they were probably tenants of William Withers as it is thought that the business was actually owned by a company which included Thomas Bright King (who is mentioned earlier in the section on the history of Chelsea Road). However none have served as long as the present incumbents - Kelvin and Penny James pictured above.

THE HORSTMANN FAMILY
(who lived at many locations in the area near their works)

Frederick Gustav Adolph Horstmann (born 1828 in Westphalia, Germany died 1893 in Bath) married Louisa Priscilla Knott (1836-1904) in 1858.
Father of:

1. Ida Matilda Agnes (1862-1946) was living with her mother and brother Sydney in 1901 and with Sydney in 1911. In 1922, 1932, and 1939 she was living with her sister Augusta at <u>77 Newbridge Road,</u> near the works entrance. They were artists and miniature painters.

2. Gustav <u>Otto</u> Henry MBE (1863-1946) married Eleanor Sarah Tarry (1860-1936). He was Chairman of Horstmann Gear Company in the 1920s and 1940s. In 1911 he was living with his wife, 5 children and brother in law at <u>19 The Vinyards</u>. In 1922 he and his wife were at <u>Forres, Newbridge Road West</u> and in 1932 they were living at <u>1 Apsley Road</u>. In 1939 he was at <u>18 Newbridge Hill</u> (as also recorded in the 1939 register). **He was father of:**

   Frederick Otto (1891-1971) in 1917 he married Amy J Goodrope (born in Broken Hill, Australia, 1894-1961), they may have had just 1 child Betty (born 1919). In 1922 was living at The <u>Woodlands, Twerton</u>, and in 1932 at <u>92 Newbridge Road</u>, In 1939 Directory he was listed at <u>14 Newbridge Road (as was Albert)</u>, In the 1939 Register, he was living at <u>Hillcot, Combe Down</u> with Companion Housekeeper Enid D Ball. His wife was then a patient at the Weston Lodge Nursing Home. In 1950 he was listed at <u>Hillcot, Horsecombe Vale.</u>

   Alfred William (1893-1927) was Head of the Gauge Department at Horstmanns, according to a newspaper report when he died.

   Kathleen Eleanor (1894-1958)

   Percival Francis (1898-1942) died at <u>The Shack, Newbridge Hill</u> with his family in Bath Blitz. He was a Departmental Manager (see page 20 above).

   Ida Louisa (1900-1987)

   Mary Josephine (1902-1967)

3. Frederick (1866-1931) married Florence Holman (1854-1933) in 1894. **He was father of:**
   Frederick George (1892); **Vida** (1898-1903); **Roxana** (1903-31).

4. Ernest Hermann (1867-1930) watch maker practical – in 1894 married Georgie Christiana Mary Henry (1865-1961). Died at Forlands, Kewstoke Road, Weston-Super-Mare leaving probate of £8117. **The 1911 census lists him as the father of:**
  G Margaret (c.1895)
  John H G (c.1896)
  Janet B (c.1898)
  Katharine (c.1899)
  Ronald B (c.1902)
  W Joyce (c.1904)
  N Patricia (c.1907).

5. Albert (1870-1957) in 1911 Census was living at 51 Newbridge Road with wife Margaret (born c.1869). In 1922 and 1932 he was living at 2 Newbridge Hill, 1939 and 1950 he was at 14 Park Lane. **He was the Father of:**
  Kenneth John (1903-1973) In 1911 Census he was living at 51 Newbridge Road with his parents and brothers Albert and Bevan but he is not in 1939 Register (perhaps he was serving in the armed services). In 1950 he was living at 14 Park Lane where he died in 1973 with probate of £248,185.
  Albert Donald (1901-1927)
  Bevan Graham (1908-1998) married Eileen A Ling (1906-99) in 1930. Until late 1930s they lived at Rusdon Cottage, Bloomfleld Road and then Ridgeway, Kingsdown, Box. *Probably had just one child: Eileen G Horstmann (1931-9).*

6. Augusta Louise (1872-1959) was living with her mother and brother Sydney in 1901 and with Sydney in 1911. In 1922, 1932, and 1939 she was living with her sister Ida at 77 Newbridge Road (see above)

7. Pauline Catherine (1878-1946) in 1903 married William Thomson Edgar. *They had no children, so far as I can find.*

8. Sydney R (1881-1962) Car manufacturer. In 1901 he was living with his mother Louise and sisters Ida and Pauline at 6 Westhall Place near Victoria Park on the Upper Bristol Road. In 1909 he married Frances Osborne (born 1880). In 1911 they were living at 10 Norfolk Crescent with his sisters Ida and Augusta, both painters, and cousin Catherine Knott. In 1922 and 1932 he and Francis were living at Omega Lodge, Albion Terrace. However in the 1939 Register they were at Fairlawn, Weston Road – and they were also there in 1950. In 1962 his probate was £37,999.

SOURCES & REFERENCES

Primary Sources
Bath Directories:
Kelly's 1914, 1919, 1923, 1927, 1950, 1970/1 and 1971/2;
Post Office 1895, 1911, 1922, 1932, 1937, 1952, 1955, 1957, 1961, 1963, 1965, 1967, 1968, 1969 and 1974
The censuses of 1891, 1901 and 1911
The 1939 Register

JH Cotterell Map of 1852
Ordnance Survey Maps 1885, 1903, 1932, 1951, 1965 and 2017
Geographia Large Scale Street Plan of Bath 1949
Bath Hacked Historical Maps at www.bathhacked.org for maps of 1795, 1818, 1852, 1885 and 1891

Publications and Websites
The Archive Photographs Series Bath by Paul De'Ath, Tempus Publishing 1995
Bath Chronicle & Herald - various articles 1890-1950
Bath Cabinet Makers - mainly Wikipedia and on-line sources
Bath Soft Cheese Company - see website: https://parkfarm.co.uk/
Bath Pubs in 1902
- see https://pubshistory.com/Somerset/Pubs1902/index.shtml
The Bath Tramways by Colin Maggs, Oakwood Press 1992
Bristol Buses & Coaches, Ian Allen Ltd., c1959
'Electricity in Bath 1890 - 1974' by William E. Eyles, Supplement to the Histelec News, December 2005
Extract from Max De Pree's Statement of Expectations for the new Herman Miller building in Bath in 1975.
Google Earth & Internet sources including Wikipedia
Grace's Guide to British Industrial History for material on Horstmann companies and Horstmann's advertisement
'A History Of Horstmann Controls' by John Perkin, South Western Electricity Historical Society Article S39, 2008
Horstman Defence Systems - website: http://www.horstman.co.uk/
Leicester University Historical Directories (Post Office 1895, 1911, Kellys 1914) www.historicaldirectories.org
Sydney Horstmann - Graces Guide, Wikipedia and Museum of Bath at Work
'Stothert & Pitt, the Rise and Fall of a Bath Company' by John Payne, Millstream Books 2007

'Charles Richter and Bath Cabinet Makers: The Early Years' Sally Festing (1998). Bath History VII: 146–166.
Commonwealth War Graves Commission website
Locksbrook Road Cemetery - the websites of The Bath Record Office, Bath & NE Somerset, Wikipedia
'Out of Nazi Germany' by Heather Tanner and Dietrich Hanff, Impact Books 1995
'The Search for Frank Pine' by John Daniels, Firs Book Spiderwize, 2016

Organisations
Bath Records Office (for extracts of many of the above directories and maps)
Bath in Time – Bath Library
Herman Miller
Rotork

Individuals
This book has been a collaborative effort involving a number of people that I have endeavoured to fully credit in my acknowledgements.

ACKNOWLEDGEMENTS

Jessica Anderson of Andrews Estate Agents for local knowledge in more recent times
Jane Brimble (nee Fudge) for the loan of Kelly's Bath 1971-72 and photographs of Newbridge School
Anya Clifton of Herman Miller for photos and material on their factories
Roger Daniels for comments and additional material
Margaret Davis for her comments
Peter De'Ath for historical photographs
Sally Festing the author, for her advice and support
Neil Garrett for advice on Farmer Kelson
John Hayden for comments and photographs
Jim Ironside for his comments
Martin James for material on Weston Bath Station (http://www.disused-stations.org.uk/w/weston_bath/)
Penny James for the history of The New Crown Inn
Stuart James for his comments
Bridget Johnston (nee Matthews) for comments and additional material, particularly on Farmer Kelson
Joyce Jones for a good deal of information, especially on the Chelsea Road bakers, and a treasure trove of photos.
Sarah Kellett Rotork Group Marketing Commutations Manager, for approval of the section on Rotork
Helen Litherland (nee Walters) for her comments and additional material including photographs
Jane Marshall for her comments
Cherry Maguire for her comments
Tony Pennington for his comments
Martin Pratt for his comments
Tony Puma for his comments
Vera Podger for her comments
Elizabeth Prevett (nee Baxter) for comments and additional material particularly extracts of Kelly's Bath 1970-71
Kirsty Pristo of CG Westminster Insurance for her comments
Peter Rubery for his comments
Philip Russell for comments and additional material
Howard Saqui for his comments
Chris Stone Bathonian's Past and Present (Facebook)
Ann White for the photograph of Joyce and Arthur Brown, 'Pop' and herself
Tony White for his Bathonians Past and Present Facebook posts

Mark Frank John Wilson for his comments and photo

Rachel Monte, legal adviser of Harper Collins (Geographia became part of Collins Bartholomew) for permission to reproduce the 1949 Geographia Plan of Bath under its 70 year copyright (the copyright of OS maps is 50 years).

The latest maps of the Chelsea Road area are © Crown Copyright 2018 and are reproduced under licence (100060009).

Stephanie Adams of Bath Records Office for advice and copies of old OS and other local maps and Bath directories.

The British Library is to be credited for the huge exercise of scanning past editions of national and local newspapers to produce a fully searchable archive. To look at articles from the Bath Weekly Chronicle & Herald, to look at articles from the Bath Weekly Chronicle & Herald, I have used the search engine at: http://www.britishnewspaperarchive.co.uk

I am indebted to Bath in Time – Bath Central Library for certain photographs reproduced in the text and the right to reproduce them.

I am generally indebted to respondents to my posts on the Bathonians pages on Facebook.

I have used my best endeavours to secure approval for the use of any material that might be copyright.

PICTURE CREDITS

Two panoramas of Chelsea Road – John Daniels 2018, Joyce Jones 1999
Newbridge Horse Bus 1890 - ©Bath in Time
Tram Newbridge Road - ©Bath in Time
My Parents - Author's collection
Twerton Footbridge - ©Bath in Time
Georges Home Brewed – Authors collection
Horstmann family - ©Bath in Time
Horstmann car - Graces Guide and Museum of Bath at Work
Horstmann advert - Graces Guide
Post Office 1960s - Bath Chronicle
Newbridge Road 1909 - Paul De'Ath
Hiskins shop in 1963 & Mr and Mrs Hiskins - ©Bath in Time
73 Newbridge Road 2018 - Google Street View in accordance with their guidelines
Chelsea Road c.1905 c.1915/16 and 1908 - Paul De'Ath
Chelsea Road 2012 - Transitions Bath
Weston Railway Station c.1910 and 1932 - John Alsop
Weston Station today - Author's collection
The Weston - pub website
Gane's last day - Joyce Jones
6 photographs of the Bakers Shop: Burris', Herbert's and Bath Bakery - Joyce Jones
2012 Picnics last day - Joyce Jones
Arthur and Joyce Brown, Pop and Ann White - Ann White
Locksbrook Cemetery - Author's collection
Locksbrook Cemetery: bronze sarcophagus with an angel by Edward Onslow Ford - Wikimedia Commons
Locksbrook Cemetery: war graves - Author's collection
Cedric Chivers Works 1984: Exterior - ©Bath in Time
Cedric Chivers Works 1984: Interior - ©Bath in Time
Cedric Chivers and Madame Sarah Grand - ©Bath in Time
Mr and Mrs Baxter - Elizabeth Prevett
The Weston Dairy - Author's collection
Norton St Philip Dairies Oldfield Park - Author's collection
Kennington Road c.1910 - Elizabeth Prevett
Walters Dairy in the 1920s, 1930s and 1962 and 1968, also Beauty Box - Helen Litherland (nee Walters)
Walters and Halls milk bottles - Mark Frank John Wilson
Pratt's 1960s - Bath Chronicle
Pratt's last day - Joyce Jones

Threshers Off Licence 1999 - Joyce Jones
Weston St John's Infant School - Author's collection
Locksbrook junction - Authors collection
Weston Magistrates Court (being pulled down in April 1961) - ©Bath in Time
Weston Tesco - Google Street View in accordance with their guidelines
Weston St John's Church (c.1900) - ©Bath in Time
Newbridge Junior School (c.1960) - ©Bath in Time
Dietrich Hanff, Robin and Heather Tanner - Impact Books
Bath City Football – Author's collection (probably Bath & West Chronicle and Herald)
Stothert & Pitt advert – Graces Guide
Bath Cabinet Makers Factory Built 1895 - Sally Festing, CC BY-SA 3.0, Wikimedia commons (family archive).
Bath Cabinet Makers (1963) - ©Bath in Time
BCM and Herman Miller Factories - Herman Miller
Rotork Headquarters - http://www.rotork.com
Chelsea Road Fun Day May 2015 - John Hayden
Newbridge Junior School 1956 and 1957 - photos by Dietrich Hanff from Jane Brimble
Kelvin and Penny James - Penny James
The New Crown Inn - Google Street View in accordance with their guidelines
Photographs of Chelsea Road 2018 - Author's collection

FEBRUARY 2018 - NEWBRIDGE ROAD
37 Old Red House B&B, 39 Former Bath Clockworks
41 Post Office, 43 Andrews Estate Agents
20 Former DorothyHouse next to former Lloyds Bank

STATION ROAD
17 Millionhairs Dog Grooming 15 Veterinery Surgery next to Genesis Gym

FEBRUARY 2018   CHELSEA ROAD   Naughty but Nice (actually 20b Newbridge Road) 1 & 2 Until 23 Dec 2016 Regency Cleaners (once Ganes & a papershop), 3 Parsons Bakery, 4 Charity Shop (was Jefferis), 5 Interior HarmonyFurnishings (once Byrts), 6 Spar Supermarket (once Windetts), 7 Justin Hunter , 7a Homecharmer (once Pennington's house)

CHELSEA ROAD   Delicatessen at 8 & 8a , 8b Chelsea Clipper, (all formerly Pennington's) 8c Greengrocers , 8d Paprika Giftware (formerly Newmans), 8e Chelsea Café (formerly the Co-op)   NEWBRIDGE HILL The New Crown Inn, Methodist Church, Cadence Bike Shop at 25 Newbridge Hill and 9 Chelsea Road (formerly a sweet shop and a fish shop)

KENNINGTON ROAD 1 CG Westminster Insurance (formerly Walters Dairy), 2 was formerly Beauty Box   CHELSEA ROAD 10 Mai Thai (formerly Halls Dairy), 11 formerly Staceys (& Grace Ironmongers), 12 Hair Studio (formerly Co-op Butchers), 13 Velopost (formerly Wise Fruiterer), 14 Sam's Barbershop (formerly Pratts), 15 Pizarella (once a drapers & then café)

16 CHELSEA ROAD Hugs Charity Shop in aid of the Royal United Hospital (since May 2013: formerly an off licence)

Next door in 1 PARK ROAD is Schmidt Kitchens & Interiors Solutions (This was formerly Mrs Ashers' Confectioners), 17 CHELSEA ROAD Formerly Speedomatic (see 2017 photo), 18 CHELSEA ROAD Beyond Beauty Salon, 20 CHELSEA ROAD (formerly 22 Newbridge Road and Luther Wilson, Chemist) Newbridge Store (convenience store)

FOXCOMBE ROAD - No 17 with its arch.

PARK ROAD The bottom of Foxcombe Road - now 45-55 Park Road (where Hortstmann's works once backed onto a wall. End of Park Road 41 and 43 (the old Horstmann's works entrance). 35, 37 and 39 Park Road. Looking along Park Road to east and then to west.

A SUMMARY OF SHOPS IN CHELSEA ROAD

Well over 40 premises have been used as shops in the area over the years but the actual numbers have fluctuated from year to year as new premises have opened, old ones have closed (as shops) or combined into single units.

	1919	1922	1932	1937	1950	1963	1970	1974	2012	2017	2018
Public House	1	1	1	1	1	1	1	1	1	1	1
Post Office	1	1	1	1	1	1	1	1	1	1	1
Baker (incl Hiskins)*	2	2	2	3	3	3	2	2	1	1	1
Grocer **	2	2	4	5	5	6	4	3		1	1
Greengrocer	2	3		2	1	1	2	2	1	1	1
Hairdresser	1	1	1	2	3	3	3	3	4	4	4
Drapers & Ladieswear	2	2	1	2	2	2	1	1			
Coal Merchant	1	1	1	1	1	1	1	1			
Shoe Repairs			1	1	1	1	1	1			
Bank		1	1	1	1	1	1	1	1		
Chemist	1	1	2	2	2	2	2	2			
Butcher	3	3	3	3	3	3	2	1			
Fishmonger	1	1	1	2	2	2	1	1			
Dairy	2	2	2	2	2	1	1	1			
Ironmonger/Hardware	1	1	1	2	2	2	2	2	1	1	1
Off Licence	1	1	1	1	1	1	2	2			
Dye Works	1	1	1	1	1						
Tobacconist			1	1	1						
Confectioners						2	3	1	1		
Fruiterer						1	1	1	1	1	1
Florist ***				1		1	1	1	1		
Restaurant/Café/Pizza						1		1	1	3	3	4
Home Furnishings							1	1	2	3	3
Estate Agent								1	2	2	2
Dry Cleaners						1	1	1	1		
Car Dealers						1	1				
Newsagent							1	1			
Launderette							1	1	1	1	
Electrical Shop						1	1	2			
Clock/Watch repair							1			1	
Supermarket								1		1	
Menswear								1			
Beauty Salon										1	1
Bike shop										1	1
Embroidery									1		
Charity									1	3	2
Giftware									1	1	1
Deli									1	1	1
Delivery Service										1	1
Insurance Office									1	1	
Second hand									2		
TOTAL	22	25	25	34	37	39	39	36	28	29	27

* Since before 1919 Hiskins bakers were at 35 (renumbered 73) Newbridge Road making it 3 bakers 1937 -1963
** Includes new convenience store 2017
*** In the last 12 years Diane Day has operated as a very good florist at the greengrocers at 8c Chelsea Road.

CENSUS DATA

1891 CENSUS - excludes any reference to: Chelsea, Kennington, Warwick, Park & Foxcombe Roads
6 Augusta Place, Lower Bristol Road, by church - Richard Canterbury, Baker & family are at Post Office

1901 CENSUS
CHELSEA ROAD (n.b. residences may also be shops)   *No records for 1, 17 etc. (not residences?)*
2 *No entry but address listed*
3 Richard Canterbury, Bread & Biscuit Baker, & family
4 John Henry Butler, Butcher, and family
5 William Ro, builder, and family
6 Richard Martin, retired builder & family - residential
7 Emma Honeyborn & niece - residential
8 Henry Brewin, Commercial Traveller, & family
9 *No entry but address listed*
10 George Ashford & Family
11 William J Scudamore, gas fitter, & family
12 George Mercer, Butcher, & wife
13 George Hayter, Greengrocer, and family
14 George Osborne, Grocers Assistant, & family
15 George Read, Draper, & wife
16 Wm Dutch, Grocer, wines etc., and family

NEWBRIDGE ROAD
113 Bloxham GP   *No records for Post Office found*
FOXCOMBE ROAD   *No records for 5,6, 9 and 21 in 1-28 sequence*
KENNINGTON ROAD *No records for 6 & 7 in 1-18 sequence*
PARK ROAD   *No records for 1 & 4 in 1-16 sequence (see*below)*
WARWICK ROAD   *Complete 1-11 sequence*

1911 CENSUS - to compare with 1919 Kellys

CHELSEA ROAD (Residences may also be shops. *No records for 1,2,9, 14, 17 etc. - not residences?)*
3 Canterbury, Baker
4 Butler, Butcher
5 Rodd, Speculative Builder
6 Seers, Master Printer
7 Frost, Lodging house
8 Pharpe, residence
10 Hall, Dairy
11 Scudamore (Sen) wife & dter, Plumber & Gasfitter
12 Brain, residence
13 Hayter, Fruiterer & Greengrocer
15 Read, Draper
16 Tresidder, Grocer

NEWBRIDGE ROAD
19 Bennett, Post Office
112 Loveless, chemist
20 Webb, Grocer

STATION ROAD
8 Jobbins, Retired Station Master, Coal Merch
15 Wood, Grocer
14 Scudamore (Jnr) wife & son, Plumber & Gasfitter
16 Redman, Station Master

FOXCOMBE ROAD   *Records for 1-28*
KENNINGTON ROAD   *Records for 1-18*
1 Charles Brown, Manager Branch Dairy, & family
PARK ROAD   *Records for 1-16 (*at variance with directories)*
WARWICK ROAD   *Records for 1-11*

KELLYS & POST OFFICE DIRECTORIES

POST OFFICE DIRECTORY 1895	POST OFFICE DIRECTORY 1911	KELLYS 1914
Station Road (numbered 1-13)	**Station Road (numbered 1-20)**	**Station Road (numbered 1-24)**
8 Jobbins, Charles, station master	8 Jobbins, Charles, coal merchant	Jobbins, Charles, coal merchant
9 Pratt A.E, grocer & wine merch	Redman, Edwin Stationmaster	Burston W Cecil, beer bottler
		Wood, Charles. grocer
Newbridge Road (no numbers)	**Newbridge Road (1-25 excl Weston hotel)**	**Newbridge Road**
Cambridge House – Dr Bloxham	113 Bloxham GE Surgeon	Cambridge House – Dr Bloxham
Fair View – EW Loveless, Chemist	112 Loveless Ed Wm, chemist	112 Loveless Ed Wm, chemist
	18 Shorney, gardener and greengrocer	18 Shorney Mrs, greengrocer
Post Office W Curtiss, stationer	19 Bennett Post Office, stationer/news	19 Bennett Post Office, stationer/news
	20 Ward & Co, Grocers and Provisions	20 Webb, Smetheram & Co, Grocers
Chelsea Road		
Station Road to Newbridge Hill		
1 Harrisson George, watchmaker	Harrisson GH, jeweller, tobacco, motor agent	Bainton Reginald, Hairdresser
2 Brice William, bootmaker	Ward & Co, grocers, etc	*No record*
3 Canterbury Richard, baker	Canterbury Mrs M J, baker	Canterbury Charles, baker
4 Butler John EL, butcher	Butler John H, butcher	Butler John Henry, butcher
5 Rodd William, sen,, builder	Rodd William, builder	*No record*
6 Martin Mr. Richard	Seers Edward H	*No record*
7 Honeybone Mrs, Emma	Frost Miss	*No record*
8 Brewin Henry, traveller	*blank*	*No record*
Newbridge Hill	**Newbridge Hill**	**Newbridge Hill**
(no nos just villas)	(nos 1-73 plus villas)	
No mention of pub	11 Crown Brewery – Beamish Alf	21 Crown Brewery Thos Burridge
		Tramway Waiting Room
9 Read George R, draper	Powell & Smith, fishmongers & poulterers	Powell & Smith, fishmongers
Pickwick Mr, George		
Kennington Road	**Kennington Road**	**Kennington Road**
Bath & Somerset Dairy (Brown C)	1. Bath & Somerset Dairy (Brown C manager)	1. Bath & Somersetshire Dairy Co
		2. Hale, Charles, decorator
10 Pickwick & Ings, grocers	Hall William, dairyman	Hall William, dairy
11 Hayter George, greengrocer	Scudamore W J, gasfitter and plumber	Scudamore W J, ironmonger
12 Chislett Mrs, E.M., butcher	Mercer G, butcher (Brain Harry, labourer)	Mercer G, butcher
13 Scudamore W, J, gasfitter	Hayter G, greengrocer, etc	Hayter G, greengrocer
14 Ashford George, dairyman	Pickwick George H, grocer	Pickwick George H, grocer
15Smith Henry, fishmonger	Read George R, draper, etc	Read George R, linen draper
Park Road (nos 1-18 listed)	**Park Road (nos 1-17 listed)**	**Park Road (Chelsea Road)**
Between Newbridge Road & NewbridgeHill!		
	Between Newbridge Road & Newbridge Hill!	
	1 Hooper Albert Ed, Newsagent	1 Hooper Albert Ed, Newsagent
		20 Rodd Wm Jun, decorator
16	Tresidder William J, grocer	Tresidder William J, grocer
	Eastmans (Ld), butchers	Eastmans (Ld), butchers
	Brook's Dye Works	Brook's Dye Works

	1919 KELLYS DIRECTORY OF BATH		1922 BATH POST OFFICE DIRECTORY
	Here is Newbridge Road- South Side: Old Nos		*Here is Newbridge Road- South Side: Old Nos*
	17 Betts Miss Ada M, Ladis Outfitter		17 Betts Miss Ada M, Fancy Draper
	Here is Station Road		*Here is Station Road*
			4 Fiddes HF Gas Company collector
	Jobbins Chas coal merchant		8 Jobbins Chas coal merchant
	Wood, Grocer		15 Wood, Grocer
			18 Parfitt Herbert, Greengrocer
	19 Post Office, Bennett Richard		19 Post Office & Stationer, Bennett RW
	20 Webb Smeteram & Co, Grocers		20 Webb & Co, Grocers
	Here is Newbridge Road -North Side: Old Nos		*Here is Newbridge Road - North Side: Old Nos*
	114 Private House - Riches Frank S		114 Lloyds Bank
	113 Bloxam G E Surgeon		113 Leckie AJ Bruce MD
	Here is Chelsea Road		*Here is Chelsea Road*
	112 Loveless William, Chemist		112 Loveless EW MPS

	Chelsea Road - East Side from South		**Chelsea Road - East Side from South**
1	Davis, Alfred Hairdresser	1	Collins, Tobacconist etc
2	Banks Edward, Greengrocer	2	Banks Edward, Greengrocer
3	Canterbury Charles, Baker	3	Canterbury Charles, Baker
4	Butler John H, Butcher	4	Butler John H, Butcher
		5	Rodd William, Builder
		6	Price John Chilton, Commercial Traveller
		7	Martin, Mrs R
		8	Phayre, Miss Annesley

	Here is Newbridge Hill		*Here is Newbridge Hill*
	21 Crown Brewery PH, Burridge Thomas		21 Crown Brewery, Burridge T
	Tramway Waiting Room (later sweet shop)		25 Bath Electric Tramways Ltd
	Wesleyan Methodist Church		Wesleyan Methodist Church

	Chelsea Road - West Side from North		**Chelsea Road - West Side from North**
9	Edwards Samuel, Fishmonger	9	Edwards John S, Fishmonger
	Here is Kennington Road		*Here is Kennington Road*
	1 Bath & Somerset Dairy Co Limited		1 Wilts & Somerset Farmers Ltd, dairy
	2 Hale Charles, Decorator		2 Hale C, Builder
	9 Gales Edwin Lesley		1-18 listed
10	Hall William J, dairy	10	Hall William J, dairyman
11	Scudamore WJ, ironmonger	11	Scudamore WJ, gasfitter
12	Mercer George, butcher	12	Mercer George, butcher
			Brain Harry, labourer
13	Shorney E A, greengrocer	13	Shorney Mrs R, greengrocer
14	Pickwick George Herbert, grocer	14	Pickwick George H, grocer
15	Williams Misses Beatrice & Mary, Draper	15	Williams Misses B&M, Draper
			Williams PW, bookbinder
	Here is Park Road		*Here is Park Road*
	Only one entry for no 26		No shops: 9-19 and 21 not errected
16	Thorley Mrs Henrietta, Beer Merchant	16	Bath Brewery Ltd, Thorley Mrs
17	Eastmans Ltd, Butcher	17	Eastmans Ltd, Butcher
18	Brooks Dye Works Ltd	18	Brooks Dye Works Ltd

Here is Newbridge Road   *Here is Newbridge Road*

NOTES

1923 KELLYS - variations from previous years
1 Collins Alfred, listed as hairdresser
   5-8 Not Listed

   Newbridge Hill -Tram Waiting Room/Parcel Depot

   26 Park Rd, Rodd Wm jun, decorator
   Station Road Burston Cecil, Beer Bottler
   113 N Road Butcher Harry H, Physician & Surgeon

1927 KELLYS - variations from previous years
1   Collins Alfred, listed as hairdresser
4   Davey Walt Edward, Butchers
13 Shorney Frank, Grocers
    25 Newbridge Hill Crown Brewery, Sydney H Ball
    1 Kennington Rd Walters John, dairyman
    2 Kennington Rd Evelyn Madame, dressmaker

    Station Road Burston & Co Wine Merchants

1932 BATH POST OFFICE DIRECTORY

Here is Newbridge Road - South Side: Old Nos

Here is Station Road

 8 Jobbins Mrs coal merchant
14A Smith Chas, Boot Repairs
15 Wood, Grocer
18 Ponting R H, Chemist
19 Post Office, Furness WT
20 Webb & Co, Grocers

Here is Newbridge Road - North Side: Old Nos
114 Lloyds Bank
113 Butcher Harry H, MRCS LRCP
  Here is Chelsea Road
112 Wilson Luther, Chemists

Chelsea Road - East Side from South
1 Collins, Tobacconist etc
2 Rule EN & Son
3 Canterbury Charles, Baker
4 Jefferis & Son, Butchers
5 Rodd Albert J, Carpenters
6 Price John Chilton, Commercial Traveller
7 Martin, Mrs R
8 *Left blank*
Here is Newbridge Hill
21 New Crown, Ball SH
25 Bath Electric Tramways Ltd
Wesleyan Methodist Church
Chelsea Road - West Side from North
9 Edwards John S, Fishmonger
Here is Kennington Road
1 Walters John, dairyman
2 Vincent Miss LA, Hairdresser
1-18 listed
10 Hall William J, dairyman
11 Scudamore WJ, gasfitter
12 Co-operative Society, Butchers
13 Shorney Frank, Grocers
14 Hiskins JH, Grocer
15 Williams Miss, Draper
Here is Park Road
1 Asher William H Plumber
1 Dover Albert
16 Thorley Mrs, Wine & Sprit Merchant
17 Eastmans Ltd, Butcher
18 Brooks Dye Works Ltd
Here is Newbridge Road

1937 BATH POST OFFICE DIRECTORY

Here is Newbridge Road - South Side: New Nos
37 Old Red House: Taylor Alfred Ltd (Bath)
  Here is Station Road
 8 Jobbins Charles coal merchant
14 Scudamore, Electrician
14a Wood, General Stores
15a Smith Chas, Boot Repairs
15b Woodham G, hairdresser
39 Ponting Reginald, Chemists
41 Post Office, Price Arthur
43 Webb F & Co, Grocers
Here is Newbridge Road - North Side: New Nos
18 Lloyds Bank, Mant CA Manager
20 Butcher Harry H, MRCS LRCP
  Here is Chelsea Road
22 Wilson Luther, Chemists

Chelsea Road - East Side from South
1 Collins, Tobacconist etc
2 Dolman EH, Fruiterer
3 Canterbury Charles, Baker
4 Jefferis & Son, Butchers
5 Byrt Wm Lionel, Fancy Drapers & Gents Wear
6 Bartlett Edmund S, grocers
7 Osborne John W, Fishmonger
Pennington Ernest Arthur, Grocer
Newman O & Sons, Ironmongers
Lake B, florists
Here is Newbridge Hill
21 New Crown, Ball SH
25 Bath Electric Tramways Ltd
Wesleyan Methodist Church
Chelsea Road - West Side from North
9 Edwards John S, Fishmonger
Here is Kennington Road
1 Walters John, dairyman
2 Vincent Miss LA, Hairdresser
1-18 listed
10 Hall William J, dairyman
11 Scudamore WJ, gasfitter
12 Co-operative Society, Butchers, Potter Dennis J, manager
13 Watts Sidney R, Greengrocer
14 Hiskins GH, Grocer
15 Williams Miss, Draper
Here is Park Road
1 Asher William H Plumber
End of south side: Park Road Garage, Culverhouse KA
16 Phillips Frdk. Russell, Wine & Sprit Merchant
17 Eastmans Ltd, Butcher
18 Brooks Dye Works Ltd
Here is Newbridge Road

THE 1939 REGISTER

OCCUPIERS RECORDED	NOTES ON PREMISES (Presumed except for 3)
NEWBRIDGE ROAD	
18 Mant, Charles A, Bank Manager, wife Edith and son John, Solicitors Clerk	Clearly Lloyds Bank
20 Butcher, Henry H, doctor and wife Yvonne	
36 Jefferis, Edith (butchers clerk), Edward and Harold	
CHELSEA ROAD	
1 No entry - presumably no residential accomodation	Probably A Collins, hairdresser, as in 1932 & 1950
2 No entry - presumably no residential accomodation	Probably Rule or Dolman Bros, greengrocers
3 Canterbury, Herbert, Baker, with wife Dorothy and 2 sons John & Michael	Canterbury's bakers shop
5 Byrt, Wiliam and wife Elizabeth, drapers	Byrt's Drapers
6 Bartlett, Edmond, wife Elizabeth and children Stanley and Muriel, grocers	Bartlett's grocers
7 Osborne John W, fish, poultry and game dealer, wife, and 3 others	Osborne, fishmongers
8 Pennington, Ernest, wife Ella, daughter Constance and son Michael	Pennington's Grocers
Type of shop premises is recorded - see final column - but no street number	Ironmongers, Newmans Ltd.
Type of shop premises is recorded - see final column - but no street number	Florists Shop, Chelsea Road
Type of shop premises is recorded - see final column - but no street number	Co-operative Store, Chelsea Road
9 No entry - presumably no residential accomodation	Presumably Edwards fish shop
10 Hall, Geoffrey, wife Hilda, 2 redacted entries, daughter Joan (later Robbins)	Hall's Dairy
11 Scudamore, William, retired, and wife (or daughter) Edith	Scudamore's Ironmongers, as in 1932 & 1950
12 Potter, Dennis J, Butchers Shop Manager, and wife Vera (and one redacted)	The Co-operative Society butchers
13 Watts, Sidney, Friut and Grocers Shop master, and wife Winifred	Watts Fruiterers in 1950
14 Carter, Sidney H, Grocery & Provisions Shop Manager, and wife, Doris	Grocers - Hiskins 1932 and 1937, Pratt's 1950
15 Cousins T and wife Getrude and 3 cabinet makers (lodging house over shop?)	Was Miss Williams drapers shop in 1932 and 1950
16 Phillips, Frederick, Licensee Off License and wife Gertrude	Off License
17 No entry - presumably no residential accommodation	Eastman's Butchers
18 No entry - presumably no residential accommodation	Brook's Dye Works
NEWBRIDGE HILL	
21 Ball, Sydney, Licensee Inn Keeper, and wife, Lydia	The Crown Inn

NOTES

The 1939 Register - pre-war - was unlike a census in many ways
But, like Censuses, it was concerned with who lived where, not businesses
So shop Premises are not generally listed and must be inferred
Addresses that are not residences are not generally listed in the register
However, in 3 instances of non-residences the shop premises are actually listed
In a large number of cases people lived over the shop, but not all owned them
Unlike censuses, relationships are not stated and must be inferred
If names are redacted the persons could be under 100 (or were still alive after 1991)
If names are listed and not redacted they were not alive in 1991

1950 KELLYS DIRECTORY OF BATH	1963 POST OFFICE DIRECTORY OF BATH
Here is Newbridge Road - South Side: New Nos	**Here is Newbridge Road - South Side: New Nos**
37 Old Red House: Taylor Alfred Ltd (Bath), Bakers	37 Old Red House: Taylor Alfred Ltd (Bath), Bakers
Here is Station Road with - on East side:	Here is Station Road with - on East side:
18 Blandford Walter, Off Licence before Ashley Ave	18 Blandford Walter, Off Licence before Ashley Ave
Jobbins, Coal Merchant, Station Yard crossing	5 Jobbins Charles, Coal & Coke Merchant
15A Smith Chas, Boot Repairs	14A Jeanette, ladies Hairdreeser
15B Woodham Gerald W, Hairdresser	15A Smith Chas, Boot Repairs
	15B Woodham Gerald W, Hairdresser
39 Ponting Reginald, Chemists	39 Ponting Reginald, Chemists
41 Post Office, George Leslie Mayne	41 Post Office and toy dealers, K&PD Beaumont
43 Webb F & Co, Grocers	43 Child RF & IBM, grocers
Here is Newbridge Road - North Side: New Nos	**Here is Newbridge Road - North Side: New Nos**
18 Lloyds Bank Ltd	18 Lloyds Bank Ltd
20 Lord William J, Doctors Surgery	20 Specimen Autos, car dealers
Here is Chelsea Road	**Here is Chelsea Road**
22 Wilson Luther, Chemists	22 Wilson Luther, Chemists
Chelsea Road - East Side from South	**Chelsea Road - East Side from South**
	Regency Cleaners & Laundry Service
1 Collins, Alfred Hairdresser	1 Skuse Maj PF, confectioners
2 Dolman Bros, Greengrocer	2 Gane PM, Greengrocers
3 Canterbury Herbert, Baker	3 Burris F, Baker
4 Jefferis E & Son, Butchers	4 Jefferis E & Son, Butchers
5 Byrt Wm Lionel, Fancy Drapers	5 Byrt Wm L, Fancy Drapers
6 Bartlett Edmund S, grocers	6 Windett & Son, grocers
7 Osborne Ja. W, Fishmonger	7 Robbies, Fishmongers
8 Pennington Ernest Arthur, Grocer	8 Pennington Ernest Arthur, Grocer
Newman O & Sons, Ironmongers	Newman O & Sons, Ironmongers
Harding Alfred G, florists	Chelsea Flower Shop (Gill & Witty)
Co-operative Retail Services Ltd	Bath Co-operative Society Ltd, provisions merchants
Here is Newbridge Hill	**Here is Newbridge Hill**
21 New Crown PH, Stanley B Crouch	21 New Crown PH
25 Murray Mrs, Confectioner	25 Ealand Mrs EJ, Confectioner
Weston Methodist Church	Weston Methodist Church
Chelsea Road - West Side from North	**Chelsea Road - West Side from North**
9 Edwards Samuel, Fishmonger	9 Edwards Samuel, Fishmonger
Here is Kennington Road	**Here is Kennington Road**
1 Walters J & Sons, dairy	1 Walters J & Sons, dairy
2 Fletcher Jn E Ladies Hairdresser	2 Eileen Ladies Hairdresser
10 Hall William J & Son, dairy	10 Silver RW, grocer
11 Scudamore William E, ironmonger	11 Grace G&I, Ironmongers
12 Bath Co-operative Society, Butchers	12 Bath Co-operative Society, Butchers
Low Herbert A	Low Herbert A
13 Watts Sidney R, Fruiterer	13 Wise MVC, Fruiterer
14 Pratt Fras L, Grocer	14 Pratt Fras L, Grocer
15 Williams Miss Beatrice, Fancy Draper	15Hawkins, Mrs AW, Drapers
Here is Park Road	**Here is Park Road**
1 Asher, confectioner (2-37 also listed with omissions)	1 Mrs ER Asher (2-37 also listed with omissions)
16Phillips Frdk R, Wine Merchant	16Hibbs Mrs LM, Wine Merchant
17Eastmans Ltd, Butcher	17 Eastmans Ltd, Butcher
18 Brooks Dye Works Ltd	18 Burge Sidney, Electrical, Radio & TV Engineer
Here is Newbridge Road	**Here is Newbridge Road**

NOTE ON CHANGES IN CHELSEA ROAD 1950-1963

Bath Post Office Directory

1952
1 Greenland, Edward, Hairdresser
2 Gane, PM Greengrocers
6 Thomas, AJ Grocer
Collyer, Mrs, Florist & Seedsman (replaced Hardings)
11 Grace, G & I, Ironmongers
15A Burge Sidney, Electrical Contractor (No shop?)

1955
7 Vote, EM Fishmonger
Chelsea Road Flower Shop, D Collyer

1957
1 Morris, Ernest L, Hairdresser
15 Bull, Mrs, Draper (Burge still at 15A)

1961
Regency Cleaners
1 Skuse, Major PF, Confectioners
3 Burris F, Bakers
6 Windett & Sons, Grocer
7 Robbie's, Fishmongers
10 Ring W, Grocer
13 Wise MVC, Fruiterer
15 Hawkins, Mrs AW, Drapers
16 Hibbs, Miss LM, Wine Merchant
18 Burge, Sidney, Electrical TV and Radio Engineer

NOTE ON CHANGES IN CHELSEA ROAD 1963-1970

Bath Post Office Directory

1965
1 Johnson AC, Newsagent
9 Batterbury G, Fishmonger
10 Hall SW, Grocer
16 Cooper, Arthur Ltd, Wine and Spirit Merchants

1967
Numbers reflect new premises built by Penningtons
8 Cavill AH, Furniture Dealers
8a Giddings HB, Watchmaker
8b Pennington EA, Grocer
(Newmans, Chelsea Flower Shop & Co-op as before)
15 Travell Mrs L, Draper
17 Speedamatic Self Service Laundry

1968
3 Homebake, Bath, Bakers
7 Sumsion F, Greengrocers
8a Giddings HB, Watch Maker

1969
6 is vacant (followed by 7 Sumsion)
7a Hibberd RJA, Shoe Repairers
(followed by 8 Cavill, 8a Giddings, 8b Penningtons, then Newmans, Chelsea Flowers and Co-op)

1970 KELLYS DIRECTORY OF BATH	1974 POST OFFICE DIRECTORY OF BATH
Here is Newbridge Road - South Side	*Here is Newbridge Road - South Side*
37 Old Red House: Taylor Alfred Ltd (Bath), Bakers	37 Old Red House: Taylor Alfred Ltd (Bath), Bakers
Here is Station Road	*Here is Station Road*
Rossiteri, Wine Merchant	Elston PE, Wine Merchant
Jobbins, Coal Merchant, Station Yard	Jobbins, Coal Merchant, Station Yard
14B Miss Newman, ladies Hairdreeser	14B Miss Newman, ladies Hairdreeser
15A Smith Chas, Boot Repairs	15A Smith Chas, Boot Repairs
15B DP Reed, Hairdresser	15B DP Reed, Hairdresser
39 Organ, Kelly & Ewance, chemists	39 Organ, Kelly & Ewance, chemists
41 Post Office and toy dealers, K&PD Beaumont	41 Post Office and toy dealers, K&PD Beaumont
43 Child RF & IBM, grocers	43 Child RF & IBM, grocers
Here is Newbridge Road - North Side	*Here is Newbridge Road - North Side*
18 Lloyds Bank Ltd	18 Lloyds Bank Ltd
20 Newbridge Motors, car dealers	20 Roberts News, newsagent
Here is Chelsea Road	*Here is Chelsea Road*
22 Wilson Luther, Chemists	22 Wilson Luther, Chemists
Chelsea Road - East Side from South	**Chelsea Road - East Side from South**
1 Johnson AC, Newsagent	1 Philip A, Menswear
2 Gane, Greengrocer	2 Gane P M, Greengrocer
3 Homebake (Bath), Bakers	3 Homebake (Bath), Bakers
4 Jefferis Harold, Butcher	4 Jefferis Harold, Butcher
5 Byrt W&L, Drapers	5 Smallworld, Fancy Drapers
6 *Left blank*	6 SPAR Supermarket
7 Parkside Greengrocers	7 Parkside Greengrocers
7a Chelsea Shoe Shop, shoe repairs	7a Chelsea Shoe Shop, shoe repairs
8 Cavill AH & Son, Furniture dirs	8 Colorwise., wallpaper and paint merchants
8a Giddings HB, watch maker	8a Moss FH (Colourvision) Ltd, television
8b Pennington EA, Grocer	8b Pennington EA, Grocer
Newman O & Sons, Ironmongers	Newman O & Sons, Ironmongers
Chelsea Flower Shop, florists	Chelsea Flower Shop, florists
Co-operative Retail Services Ltd	Co-operative Retail Services Ltd
Here is Newbridge Hill	*Here is Newbridge Hill*
Crown Inn Public House	Crown Inn Public House
Methodist Church	Methodist Church
Chelsea Road - West Side from North	**Chelsea Road - West Side from North**
9 Battersbury, Fishmonger	9 Swifts, fishery
Here is Kennington Road	*Here is Kennington Road*
1 Walters G D B, dairyman	1 Walters G D B, dairyman
2 Beauty Box, Ladies Hairdresser	2 Beauty Box, Ladies Hairdresser
10 Nell Gwyn, Restaurant	10 Nell Gwyn, Restaurant
11 Grace, Ironmongers	11 Clare's, Hardware
12 Co-operative Retail Services Ltd	12 May, Stanley
13 Wise MVC, Fruiterer	13
14 Pratt Fras L, Grocer	14 Pratt Fras L, Grocer
15	15
Here is Park Road	*Here is Park Road*
1 Mrs El Asher, confectioner	1 Mrs El Asher, confectioner
16 Cooper Arthur Ltd, Wines & Spirits	16 Cooper Arthur Ltd, Wines & Spirits
17 Speedamatic, Self Service Laundry	17 Speedamatic, Self Service Laundry
18 Burge Sidney, Radio & TV Engineer	18 Burge Sidney, Radio & TV Engineer
Here is Newbridge Road	*Here is Newbridge Road*

November 2012 Transition Report Appendix 1: Businesses on Chelsea Road and at the junction with Newbridge Road *(with my comments on the position in 2018)*

	Category	Company Nov 2012	2018
1	Bank	Lloyds TSB	Closed 2017 now offices
2	Bakery	Bath Bakery	Now Parsons Bakers
3	Beauty Salon	Beyond Beauty	
4	Bicycle Shop	Cadence	
5	Café	Chelsea Café	
6	Café and Delicatessen	Chelsea Road Delicatessen	
7	Charity Shop	Mercy in Action	
8	Clock Repairs	Clockworks	Closed
9	Dental Specialist	Dental Implant Clinic	
10	Drycleaners	Regency Drycleaners	Closed Dec 2016
11	Embroidery Service	Bath Embroidery Service	Closed Dec 2016
12	Estate Agents	Andrews	
13	Estate Agents	Justin Hunter	
14	Flooring Shop	Interior Harmony Flooring	
15	Florist	Flowers of Perfection	
16	General Stores	Newbridge Stores	
17	Gift Shop and Furnishings	Window Dressing	Closed now Paprika
18	Hairdresser	No 12	
19	Hairdresser	Chelsea Clipper	
20	Hairdresser	Naughty But Nice	
21	Hairdresser Men's	Sam's Barber	
22	Hardware Shop	Homecharmer	
23	Kitchen Design Shop	Interior Harmony Kitchen	
24	Launderette	Speedamatic Laundry	Closed 2018
25	Motor Insurance Westminster Motor Insurance	Westminster Motor Insurance	Closed
26	Optician	Armstrong & North	Closed now Velopost
27	Post Office	Post Office	
28	Pub	New Crown	
29	Second Hand Furniture Shop	Inandated Furniture (was at 20 Newbridge Road before Dorothy House)	Closed now Rooted Cafe
30	Second Hand Furniture Shop	Stacey's Quality Used Goods (then Stacey's TV & Video at 11 Chelsea Rd)	Closed
31	Small Supermarket	Spar	
32	Surveyors	Hurst Associates 22 Newbridge Road	
33	Surveyors	Lamberts Building Surveyors Limited 7 Chelsea Road	
34	Takeaway and Restaurant	Desh	Closed now Mai Thai
35	Takeaway Pizza	Pizzarella	
36	Vegetable Shop	The Greengrocer	

2017 GOOGLE EARTH STREET VIEW & INTERNET SEARCHES   CHANGES BY 2018

	Here is Newbridge Road - South Side	
	37 Old Red House B&B	
	Here is Station Road	
	17 Millionhairs Dog Grooming before Ashley Ave	
	15 Station Road Veterinary Surgery	
	39 Bath Clockworks (watch and clock repairs)	Vacant – for sale
	41 Post Office	
	43 Andrews Estate Agents	
	Here is Newbridge Road - North Side	
	18 Newbridge Road - now an office	
	20 Newbridge Road, Dorothy House, next to former Lloyds Bank	Vacant – for sale
	20b Newbridge Road (actually in Chelsea Raod) Naughty but Nice, Hairdressers	
	Here is Chelsea Road	
	22 Newbridgestore (as for Luther Wilson – now 20 Chelsea Road)	
	Chelsea Road - East Side from South	
1	Bath Embroidery Services now up for sale	Vacant – for sale
2	Regency Cleaners now up for sale	Vacant – for sale
3	Parsons Bath Bakery	
4	Charity Shop	
5	Interior Harmony Flooring	
6	Spar Goss Supermarket	
7	Justin Hunter, Estate Agent	
7a	Homecharmer	
8	The Chelsea Road Delicatessen	
8a		
8b	Chelsea Clipper	
8c	The Chelsea Road Greengrocers	
8d	Paprika	
8e	The Chelsea Café	
	Here is Newbridge Hill	
	East side of Chelsea Road The New Crown Inn at 21 Newbridge Hill	
	Chelsea Road - West Side from North	
9	Cadence Bike Shop (incorporates old Sweet Shop Newbridge Hill)	
	Here is Kennington Road	
	1 CG Westminster Insurance	Vacant
	2 Beauty Box premises can still be seen	
10	Desh Indian Restaurant	Mai Thai restaurant
11	Staceys TV and Video Sales	Vacant – for sale
12	No 12 Hair Studio	
13	Armstrong & North Optician	Velopost bicycle delivery service
14	Sams Barber Shop	
15	Pizzarella	
	Here is Park Road	
	1 Schmidt Kitchen Design	
16	HUGS - Help Us Give Support (for RUH)	
17	Speedamatic, Self Service Laundry	Vacant – for sale
18	Beyond Beauty	

See above for 20 Chelsea Road – formerly 22 Newbridge Road: Newbridgestore

THE CHALLENGES OF ROAD NUMBERING

CHELSEA ROAD - Chelsea Road was originally numbered 1-8 on the east side and 9-18 on the west side:but when a gap was filled on the east side the new building was numbered 8a-e. Newbridge Store, formerly 22 Newbridge Road is now 20 Chelsea Road, but Naughty but Nice is 20b Newbridge Road.

NEWBRIDGE HILL - In 1895 none of the houses in Newbridge Hill were numbered - the houses all had names. By 1911 the houses were numbered sequentially from the junction with Newbridge Hill at the Weston Hotel so that The Crown Brewery (The New Crown) was number 11. By 1914 Newbridge Hill was numbered (as now) with odd numbers on the south side so that The Crown Brewery was 21 and even numbers on the north side starting at Combe Park.

NEWBRIDGE ROAD WAS ENTIRELY RENUMBERED IN THE MID 1930s - Originally Newbridge Road was numbered omitting the Weston Hotel and the next property and continued on the south side to two houses after Osborne Road and then continued back from Rosslyn Road on the north side. So (given one omission) comparisons are complicated:

1932	1937
South Side From Bath	**South Side From Bath - Odd Nos**
Weston Hotel	1 Weston Hotel
Spencers Garage	3 Spencers Garage
1-16 Newbridge Road	5-35 Newbridge Road
17 Newbridge Road	37 Old Red House
18 Ponting Chemist	39 Ponting Chemist
19 Post Office	41 Post Office
20 Webb Grocers	43 Webb Grocers
21-34 Newbridge Road	45-71 Newbridge Road
35 Hiskins John, Baker	73 Hiskins Stanley, Baker
36-76 Newbridge Road	75-155 Newbridge Road
77 Rodd, Mason	157 Rodd, Mason
North Side to Bath	**North Side to Bath -Even Nos**
78-90 Newbridge Road	88-64 Newbridge Road
91 Newbridge Road	Omitted (works entrance?)
92 Horstman Fredk O	62 Horstmann Gear Co
93-4 Horstman Gear Co	60-58 Horstmann Gear Co
95-111 Newbridge Road	56-24 Newbridge Road
112 Wilson Luther, Chemist	22 Wilson Luther, Chemist
113 Butcher, doctor	20 Butcher, doctor
114 Lloyds Bank	18 Lloyds Bank
115-122 Newbridge Road	16-2 Newbridge Road

153 is now 'Just 4 Bath' Off Licence & Grocery – it was run by Harry and John Miles as a newsagents in the 1960s

155 & 157 are across Osborne Road

88 Now Hawkins Guest House west of Rosslyn Road

Newbridge Road Continues to Newton
90-176 (178-188 not built)
190-194
202-208 (210-216 not built)
218-236 Post Office

PARK ROAD WAS NUMBERED WITH A VIEW TO BUILDING ROWS OF TERRACE HOUSES - So there were gaps that were only partly in-filled with semi-detached houses after the war - and, at the start of this century, new houses were built as 39-55 (although 41 and 43 are aligned with Foxcombe Road where there had been the Horstmann's works' entrance and 45-55 continue up along Foxcombe Road).

PARK ROAD	1923 to now			
North Side Even Numbers	2 to 26			
	1922-1937	By 1950	By 1963-1970	By 2017
South Side Odd Numbers	1 to 7, 23 to 33	1 to 7, 23 to 37	1 to 15, 23 to 37	1 to 15, 23 to 55
Not Built	9 to 21, over 33	9 to 21, over 37	17 to 21, over 37	17 to 21

www.ingramcontent.com/pod-product-compliance
Lightning Source LLC
LaVergne TN
LVHW070013090426
835508LV00048B/3381